I0561049

Nicholas Smith

Stories of great national songs

Nicholas Smith

Stories of great national songs

ISBN/EAN: 9783337266165

Printed in Europe, USA, Canada, Australia, Japan

Cover: Foto ©Thomas Meinert / pixelio.de

More available books at **www.hansebooks.com**

STORIES OF

GREAT NATIONAL SONGS

—BY—

COLONEL NICHOLAS SMITH.

" I knew a very wise man, so much of Sir Christopher's sentiment, that he believed if a man were permitted to make all the ballads, he need not care who should make the laws of a nation."

—Andrew Fletcher, of Salton.

MILWAUKEE, WIS.:
THE YOUNG CHURCHMAN CO.,
And 7-9 West 18th Street, New York.
LONDON:
SAMPSON LOW, MARSTON & CO.

To
The Wife of My Youth
Whose Devotion and Encouragement
Have Been a Constant Benediction,
This Volume is
Lovingly Dedicated.

Acknowledgments.

THE author takes pleasure in expressing his indebtedness to the John Church Company of Cincinnati, for the use of the excellent portrait of Dr. George F. Root, and the words of two of his war songs; to that comprehensive and valuable work, "Our War Songs, North and South," published by S. Brainard's Sons, Cleveland, for the words of several songs and the portrait of Charles C. Sawyer; to Champlin's monumental "Cyclopedia of Music and Musicians," published by Charles Scribner's Sons, for the portrait of Rouget de Lisle; and to J. F. Kreh of Frederick, Md., for the beautiful illustration of Key's monument.

Contents.

Illustrations.

STORIES OF

GREAT NATIONAL SONGS

I.

Illustrations of the Power of Song.

TWO hundred years ago, Andrew Fletcher, of
Salton, the noted Scottish patriot, said: "I
knew a very wise man, so much of Sir
Christopher's sentiment, that he believed if a man
were permitted to make all the ballads, he need not
care who should make the laws of a nation." A
writer of unknown name, in commenting on this
famous, but usually misquoted saying, suggests
that the wise man did not mean to disparage
statesmanship, but to emphasize the fact that
songs accepted by the people as expressions of national sentiment have a far greater influence than
the statutes enacted to carry out given political
doctrines and purposes.

It is easy to trace through the history of civilization the subtle force of popular melodies representing thoughts and emotions that have prevailed from time to time, and helped to shape the course of events. There seems to be something in human nature which demands a musical outlet for certain forms of patriotic and religious feeling. "And all countries have their favorite and characteristic songs, corresponding to the temperament and tendency of their respective peoples. There has never been a country on earth so poor that it did not have at least one simple ballad, dear to the common heart, and serving as a source of inspiration in time of peril."

There is no higher human power than music. It will move men's souls when the mightiest of orators fail. A few years ago some one watched the most noted infidel in the world, Colonel Robert G. Ingersoll, as he listened to that great master, Remenyi, drawing his wondrous bow upon his violin. Those marvelous strains soon touched the overflowing heart of the famous agnostic, and as the big tears fell "from the eye that had so often flashed with scorn," everybody present felt as never before, the striking wonder of the pathos, beauty and power of music. There is something like a divine influence in music, and

that explains why birds of prey never sing, and
infidelity has no song.

Mr. Henry T. Finck, in an article on "The
Utility of Music," printed in a recent number of
The Forum, speaks about music superseding the
chime bells in calling people to worship. In some
parts of Germany, especially at Stuttgart, they
have a more delightful and effective way of drawing people to church than by the clanking of the
bells. Three or four trombone-players enter the
church tower a short time before the hour of service and play a solemn choral so sweetly that the
charm and purifying joy in the majestic harmonies wafting in the air, are not wasted on dull
ears, but impress passers-by with the fact that
Sunday is not as a sponge with which to wipe out
the follies of the week, but a day of worship, and
many hundreds are drawn to the service who
would otherwise pass by the church door.

Music has had more to do in soothing the
stormy and bitter passions of mankind, in elevating their thoughts, in exciting their sympathies,
than any other agency of man's invention; and
how many times "the contrary stream of thought,
and opinion, and feeling, and impulse, have been
united by song in an ocean of good will and mutual
helpfulness."

The greatest intellects are those that can inter-
pret and reveal man's own soul; and herein lies
the power of the world's great poets and musicians.
An incident which illustrates how quickly the
human heart responds to genuine soul song, is a
touching scene in the life of Jenny Lind. The
sweet singer of Sweden, whose smile, as well as
voice, was the most heavenly ever given to woman,
was, at the height of her renown, singing in London. Giulia Grisi, Italy's "singing flower of
beauty," was also in London winning much popular applause. Both were invited to sing the same
night at a court concert before the Queen. Jenny
Lind being the younger, sang first, and was so dis-
turbed by the fierce, scornful look of Grisi, that she
was at the point of failure, when suddenly an inspiration came to her. The accompanist was striking his final chords. She asked him to rise, and
taking the vacant seat, her fingers wandered
over the keys in a loving prelude, and then she
sang a little prayer which she had loved as a child.
She had not sung it for years. As she sang she
was no longer in the presence of royalty, but singing to loving friends in her fatherland.

Softly at first the plaintive notes floated on the
air, swelling louder and richer every moment. The
singer seemed to throw her whole soul into that

weird, thrilling, plaintive "prayer." Gradually
the song died away and ended in a sob. There
was silence—the silence of admiring wonder. The
audience sat spellbound. Jenny Lind lifted her
sweet eyes to look into the scornful face that had
so disconcerted her. There was no fierce expression now; instead, a teardrop glistened on the
long, black lashes, and after a moment, with the
impulsiveness of a child of the tropics, Grisi
crossed to Jenny Lind's side, placed her arm about
her and kissed her, utterly regardless of the
audience.

By the power and influence of their songs men
and women have made possible the mightiest
evangelistic movements of the centuries. They
have revolutionized parties, and have changed the
history of nations. The importance of songs and
ballads in effecting great changes in national life,
whether reformatory, revolutionary, or religious,
is shown in the history of almost every country on
the globe.

Sir George Grove, in his Dictionary of Music,
gives an interesting account of the Italian song,
"Daghela avanti un Passo," which means, "Move a
step forward." It is a striking exemplification of
the tremendous power of popular song. In 1858
Milan was a hotbed of Italian conspiracy and in-

trigue against the Austrian rule in Lombardy. At the Teatro della Cannobiana a ballet dancer was received by the spectators with mingled applause and hisses. This gave rise to disorder; the police interfered and took the part of the majority, who were averse to the dancer. At once the popular sympathies were enlisted in her favor, and her cause was henceforth identified with patriotic aspirations.

Further disturbances followed and the run of the ballet was stopped, but the tune to which the ballet girl danced her passo, a solo, passed into the streets of Milan and was heard everywhere. The words, partly Italian, partly Milanese, were a hybrid melange of love and war, with the refrain, "Daghela avanti un passo." This was received by the public as an exhortation to patriotic action, while by the Austrians both tune and words were deemed an insolent challenge and were not forgotten a few months later when war was declared between Austria and the Kingdom of Piedmont. "Daghela avanti" was then played in derision by the Austrian military bands as they advanced into Piedmont, just as "Yankee Doodle" was played by the British bands in ridicule of the American colonists during the French and Indian war previous to the Revolution. But Austria was soon obliged to evacuate Piedmont, and her retreating armies heard the same strains sung by the advancing soldiers of Italy. Province after province was annexed to Piedmont, and with each successive annexation the popularity of this strange song increased until it was heard all over Italy.

Probably no other song, not patriotic or religious, ever had a more marvelous career than Thomas Hood's "Song of the Shirt," written in 1843. In its power to touch the emotions and arouse men to action, it counted for more than all else Hood ever wrote. It not only "ran through the land like wildfire," but in the great strikes that seemed to shake England to her center, it had an incomparable controlling influence. It became so popular that it was translated into German, French and Italian. It was printed on cotton handkerchiefs by the hundreds of thousands, and was parodied times without number. That which touched Tom Hood most deeply, because he never thought the song was very remarkable, was that the poor men and women and boys and girls, whose sorrows and sufferings were many, seemed the happier when going about the street singing the "Song of the Shirt" to a rude melody of their own composition.

It is said there would be no difficulty in put-

ting together the history of England in its boldest
outlines from the songs inspired by the great crises
through which the nation has passed. The songs
of the civil war of that country were a series of
political ballads which, for personality and power,
still remain unrivalled. It was a war whose fierce-
ness was as much due to song as to the sword; and
history tells us that song, perhaps more than any
other outside influence, brought the head of
Charles I. to the block. We are told that "the
musicians who led Napoleon's old guard to doom
and destruction on the last day at Waterloo, will
possibly have to answer for more reckless murders
when the record of bloody deeds are read beyond
the stars, than any of the generals who exchanged
the compliments of the season on that historic occasion, for it is said somewhere in history that when
the greatest general the world ever saw gave up
in doubt and discouragement on that day, the
'band played on.' " Men eagerly marched to the
field of slaughter by the impelling strains of the
"Marseillaise."

One of the most interesting and remarkable
events ever known in the history of our government
showing the power of a simple song, was the great
political storm which swept over this country in
1840. In that year there lived at Zanesville, Ohio,

Alexander C. Ross,

AUTHOR OF THE FAMOUS "TIPPECANOE AND TYLER TOO."

a young business man, Alex. C. Ross by name, who was fuller of Whig enthusiasm than of fine poetry; and one Sunday morning, very early in the famous campaign, while sitting in the church choir, Mr. Ross' feelings found expression in those easy-going and catchy words, "Tippecanoe and Tyler Too," adapted to the tune of "Little Pigs;" and in a month the song seemed to have traversed the Union. Steady-going merchants, sober-minded business men, lawyers and doctors, and statesmen and ministers, joined with wonderful enthusiasm in the log-cabin and hard-cider music; and it is a bold fact that in that campaign a president of the United States was sung into the White House by the chorus of "Tippecanoe and Tyler Too;" the song exerting an influence entirely beyond the reach of speeches and newspapers.

Song writers are political, social and religious reformers. They have stirred mankind profoundly by the sweeping, conquering inspiration of their songs, ballads and hymns. These products of the heart—a source whence come all great songs—are so universal in their use, and have such mysterious power, that some one has said that "not until we know why the rose is red, the dewdrop pure, and the rainbow beautiful, can we know why the song-poet is the best benefactor of humanity." Frances

E. Willard has told us that no names are deathless save those of the world's singers; and whoever weds perfect music to noblest words soothes the world's heart as no other can. And it is one of the impressive facts of history that they who make the songs of the church wield a vaster power than they who build her creeds.

A correspondent of the "Musical Age," writing from Porto Rico early in the autumn of 1898, says:

"You will never be able to appreciate what a godsend to the human race the banjo is until you come down here, and, strolling out of an evening, hear the hundreds of them being played in the camp. You cannot conceive what a blessing this little half-musical instrument is to the soldiers. The day is full of activity for them, but in the evening there is nothing to do, and in the half-way tide of friendship there is little pleasure in conversation. But when five hundred banjos play 'Home, Sweet Home,' all together, the croaking of the frogs sounding dreamily and comfortably through the interludes, you begin to feel very emotional, and to appreciate that emotion is a fine thing now and then, and that the banjo is a very much misunderstood instrument."

In the realm of war songs we find the be-

ginning of the poetry of every nation. There
is almost supreme wonderment in the battle hymn
when studied as to its influence in early times
on history. Among our northern ancestry the
highest salvation was reserved for him who died
by the sword; and the fire which caused the blaze
—the burning life of those terrible conquests,
whose war-flames lighted all Europe, was the thrilling power of war songs. Those lyrics were the
outburst of patriotism and the inspirer of courage;
and the degree to which the mere words of a song
maddened the Norsemen, and drove them to tremendous deeds during many stormy centuries, is
shown in every chapter of their history, and in
every life of their heroes; for the song was to them
sermon and newspaper, oration and argument, law
and promise, all in one. We are told that these
anthems of war were sung by bards in the fiercest
tones, and that their influence on the history of
Scandinavia reads like one loud call to battle.

The popularity and power of some of those old
war songs of centuries ago can hardly be under-
stood in our time. A few years ago an article
appeared in The Nineteenth Century which gave
instance of the influence of song in shaping the
destinies of some of the European countries. "By
a thousand facts," the article says, "we know that

it was the Teutonic war song which led to the destruction of Rome ; the same means shattered the civilization of Southern Europe, and expurgated the corruption of the oriental influence, and in time led to the era of the Middle Ages and the Crusades."

But what I desire to give in these pages is the story of patriotic songs, and more particularly to illustrate and illuminate the controlling power of the great battle-hymns of the Union. The sacred fire which has burned on the altar of patriotism has flamed into many priceless songs, some of which will forever remain among the most potent influences known to the great nations of the world. Such songs were born of the greatest moments of the singers and the times. When the civil war began, the land swarmed with singers. They were not all good, but the best of them will live as long as the flag. From Julia Ward Howe's brave words in the "Battle Hymn of the Republic," to the negro melodies of the far South, the pean of courage went up. Observant people said that a nation which could sing such songs at such a time was already assured of victory. The story of these songs of the Union warms the blood, stimulates patriotism, and teaches American youth that they have a heritage of glory beyond the power of tongue to tell.

Yankee Doodle.

FROM THE PAINTING BY WILLARD, NOW IN THE ABBOTT HALL, MARBLEHEAD, MASS.

II.

The First American National Air—
"Yankee Doodle."

AMERICA, with a national life of a little more than a century, has produced some battle songs of powerful and permanent influence. When the revolution began there was no song for the colonists to sing. A national hymn, as well as a national flag, was lacking. "Music is the universal language of emotion." It gives vent to excitement. There is a charming eloquence in verse, and the strong feeling of great numbers always tends to utterance in song.

The history of American national airs begins with a breezy, good-natured sort of a tune, that men often laugh at, but which has been a conquering power in five wars, and is known by the familiar and eccentric title of "Yankee Doodle." How, when, or where the tune first came into use, nobody knows. It is a good deal like Topsy, "it was never born, but growed." The words, adapted to the music and commonly used in the Revolutionary war, were the product of those stirring times, but to attempt to write the history of the tune would be nothing less than bewildering. There is as much amazing obscurity surrounding the origin of "Yankee Doodle" as there is uncertainty connected with the airs to which we sing "My Country, 'Tis of Thee," and "John Brown's Body Lies a Mouldering in the Grave." But, inasmuch as the tune once made a big stir in the world, and rapidly rose from a composition of reproach to one of triumph and rejoicing, and is too priceless a heritage for Americans to disown or disuse, it will be interesting, perhaps, as well as curious, to look briefly into its peculiar history.

Benson J. Lossing, that master in everything of importance concerning revolutionary times and men, tells us that the air Nancy Dawson—which, by the process of evolution, became known as Yankee Doodle—antedates the American Revolution by at least one hundred and twenty-five years. It was during Cromwell's time, it is said, that some rustic bard broke out in a song that began—

Nankey Doodle came to town,
  Riding on a pony,
  With a feather in his hat,
  Upon a macaroni,

and sung to the redoubtable tune of "Yankee Doodle."

It is also said that in the reign of Charles I., the Puritans, who wore their hair cut short, were nicknamed Roundheads by the Cavaliers, or Royalists, who wore their hair in long ringlets. The term Yankee, or Nankey, was applied in contempt to the Puritans of simple ways, by the proud followers of the unfortunate Charles. The word Yankee is defined in several ways. The Century Dictionary of Names, while considering the origin of Yankee uncertain, says that according to a common statement, "Yankees" is a variation of "Yenkees," or "Yengees," or "Yaunghees," a name said to have been given by Massachusetts Indians to the English colonists, being, it is supposed, an Indian corruption of the word English. Some attempt has been made to disprove the Cromwellian origin of the tune and words, but without result in giving a clearer or more reasonable account of either. The word Doodle is defined in the old English dictionaries to be a trifling, or simple fellow, and the term was applied to Cromwell, so it is claimed, in that sense; and a macaroni was a knot on which the feather was fastened.

But again referring to the word Yankee, there is a story told that a farmer of Cambridge, Mass., named Jonathan Hastings, who lived about the year 1713, used it as a favorite cant word to express excellence, as a yankee good horse or yankee good cider. The students of Harvard college, hearing him use it a good deal, adopted it and called him Yankee Jonathan, and as he was rather a weak man, the students, when they wished to denote a character of that kind, would call him a Yankee Jonathan. Like other cant words, it spread and came finally to be applied to the New Englanders as a term of reproach.

It is the consensus of opinion among those entitled to a hearing in this matter, that "Yankee Doodle," which has long since become an American national air without words, is several hundred years old, and had its beginning either in England, Spain, Hungary, or Holland. Recently the New York Sun printed an article to prove that the tune was commonly used among the Spaniards long before it emigrated to America.

In Duyckinck's Cyclopedia of American Literature the statement is made that a song was in use among the laborers, who in the time of harvest,

migrated from Germany to the low countries of
Holland, where they received for their work as
much buttermilk as they could drink and a tenth of
the grain secured in the harvest, which began with
the verse—sung to the tune of "Yankee Doodle"—

> "Yankee didel, doodel down,
> Didel, dudel lanter,
> Yanke viver, voover vown,
> Botermilk and Tanther."

That is, buttermilk and a tenth. While this
narrative has been reproduced approvingly in
Littell's Living Age, and in many other distinguished publications, philologists say that the
words made to answer the purpose of a harvest
song as just quoted, are not found in any known
language in the low countries of Holland or anywhere else, which is good authority for supposing
that such a story cannot be safely taken as history.

The story of "Yankee Doodle" from the time it
was brought to this country is definite, and absorb-
ingly interesting. It has had a great mission.
With all the derision that has been heaped upon it,
it is none the less a great tune. When one hears
the once ridiculed and rollicksome strains of
"Yankee Doodle" let him cogitate the fact that it
has been the marching tune of all the victorious
armies of American patriots, and has such a

universal sentiment and universal nationality, that it will measure the tread of coming millions. It is one of the indestructible institutions of America. It has a character of its own—comical, rampant, "rattle-brainish," but with all its oddities, it has somehow entwined itself so closely about the national heart that one might as well try to rob the people of the American bicycle, or Bunker Hill, as this "clattering, right-about-face, defiant battle march."

The tune was brought to this country in 1755 when the British were engaged in a war with the French and Indians. The story goes that the militia which were called to aid the British regular army were strangely clad in many colors, some wearing long coats, some short ones, and many having none of any kind to wear. In the British army was one Dr. Richard Shackburg, who not only mended shattered limbs, but was somewhat of a musician. One day he thought to play a joke upon the militia because of their grotesque figure and awkward manner, and with much mock solemnity he presented them the words and music of "Yankee Doodle," commending the tune as one of the most distinguished in martial music. The joke greatly pleased the well dressed British officers, but as a joke it proved a stupendous failure, for the tune soon became the battle march of the Revolution. They who laugh last laugh best. The British officers would raise shouts of laughter when they heard the innocent and simple-minded militia play "Yankee Doodle," and the British bands would repeat it in derision of the colonists. This contemptuous use of the song by the English army continued more than twenty years; then came the battle of Lexington, and by a strange irony of fate, the colonists made the British dance to the tune of "Yankee Doodle." The giving of the tune to the ill-circumstanced militia in mockery of their unfortunate appearance, was a prophetic piece of fun, for twenty-five years later Lord Cornwallis was forced to march to the tune of "Yankee Doodle" when entering the lines of the same colonists to surrender his sword and his army to General Washington.

There were innumerable songs adapted to the tune of "Yankee Doodle" just previous to and during the Revolutionary war; and one of them began—

> "Yankee Doodle is the tune
>   Americans delight in:
> 'Twill do to whistle, sing or play,
>   And is just the thing for fighting."

But the original "Yankee Doodle" words which became the song of the Revolution, are said to have been written by a Connecticut gentleman, and it seems that fate did him a kindness by concealing his name. There were sixteen stanzas including the chorus, and the title of the composition was "Yankee Doodle: or Father's Return from Camp." It is hardly less than a jumble of almost idiotic lines, and the hilarious spirit of those times, and the burlesque character of the song which created such a sensation on two continents, can be best illustrated by sacrificing space to all the stanzas:

> Father and I went down to camp,
>   Along with Cap'n Good'n,
> And there we saw the men and boys
>   As thick as hasty puddin'.

CHORUS:
> Yankee doodle, keep it up,
>   Yankee doodle dandy
> Mind the music and the step,
>   And with the girls be handy.

> And there we see a thousand men,
>   As rich as 'Squire David;
> And what they wasted every day
>   I wish it could be saved.

> The 'lasses they eat every day
>   Would keep a house in winter;
> They have so much that I'll be bound
>   They eat it when they're mind ter.

And there I see a swamping gun,
    Large as a log of maple,
Upon a deuced little cart
    A load for father's cattle.

And every time they shoot it off
    It takes a horn of powder,
And makes a noise like father's gun,
    Only a nation louder.

I went as nigh to one myself
    As 'Siah's underpinning;
And father went as nigh again,
    I thought the deuce was in him.

Cousin Simon grew so bold
    I thought he would have cocked it;
It scared me so I shrinked it off
    And hung by father's pocket.

And Cap'n Davis had a gun,
    He kind o' clapped his hand on't,
And stuck a crooked stabbing iron
    Upon the little end on't,

And there I see a pumpkin shell
    As big as mother's basin,
And every time they touched it off
    They scampered like the nation.

I see a little barrel, too,
    The heads were made of leather;
They knocked on it with little clubs
    To call the folks together.

And there was Cap'n Washington
    And gentle folks about him;
They say he's grown so 'tarnal proud
    He will not ride without 'em.

He got him in his meeting clothes
Upon a slapping stallion;
He set the world along in rows
In hundreds and in millions.

The flaming ribbons in his hat
They looked so tearing fine, ah,
I wanted dreadfully to get
To give to my Jemima.

\ I see another snarl of men
A-digging graves, they told me,
So 'tarnal long, so 'tarnal deep,
They 'tended they should hold me.

'. It scared me so I hooked it off,
Nor stopped, as I remember,
Nor turned about, till I got home,
Locked up in mother's chamber.

There is some disagreement as to the date of
these words, one authority claiming that they first
appeared in 1765, but the general opinion appears
to be that they were written about 1775, as the first
recorded account is of their being sung at the
battle of Bunker Hill.

Compared with the later battle songs of the
Union, "Yankee Doodle" dwindles into an aggre-
gation of senseless stanzas, but its remarkable
popularity and power at a time when the American
colonists were making the supreme effort for
independence closely link it with imperishable
historical associations.

III.

Billings—The First American War Song Writer.

THE quaintest character that appears among the makers of American war songs was William Billings, who was born in Boston, in 1746, and died in the same city in 1800. The story of his life has a peculiar interest for the reason that he was the earliest native writer of music in America. He was zealous in the cause of liberty, and the patriotic ardor which characterized his songs and tunes made them a power among the colonists. The New England soldiers, who, during the war of the Revolution, were stationed in the Southern States, committed many of his tunes to memory, and amused themselves by singing them in camp to the delight of all who heard them.

This Yankee composer of psalm tunes, anthems, and writer of army songs, should not be judged by the musical standard of the nineteenth century. Flippant critics of the new school of music have tried to make much fun of him because he had neither a musical nor literary education. He was a genius, a "diamond in the rough," and it has been said by some one that Billings' works have survived their critics, "and are sung in grateful recollection by thousands over all the land, while forgetfulness covers his detractors."

In his day, and according to his opportunities, Billings was a great success. He was taught the business of a tanner, and worked at the trade for a number of years. He was born with music in his soul, and quite early in his young manhood began to sing, then to teach, and finally to write words and compose music for church people and the colonial army. Of course, he was an "awkward harmonist," a "worse contrapuntist," his "technique" was deficient, his "consecutive fifths" were out of joint, his "progressions of octaves" were illogical, and his chords and harmonies were tumbled together without order, but he roused the people by his songs, and was the great musical missionary of his time.

Billings was a man of rare spiritual earnestness, and his patriotism was as fervid as his religious nature was intense. Dr. Frederic

Louis Ritter, in his "Music in America," says: "The American Revolution caused the colonists to turn against everything that was British. The innocent old psalm tunes received a part of the momentary patriotic hatred; and with the tea the British tunes were also thrown overboard." Billings was the man of the time with "the genius and zeal to write words and music that moved the hearts and nerved the arms to strike for freedom in those early days." He assumed the task of furnishing words and music to take the place of those which had gone overboard with the tea. He became the singer of the army and the psalmist of the church. His superior inventive genius and his ever glowing enthusiasm, enabled him to supply music for almost every occasion. One of his popular songs was written for the special use of the army, although it was taken up by the people and became an inspiring force. It was set to the tune of "Chester," his own composition, an air that was frequently heard from every fife in New England. The readers can obtain a tolerably fair idea of the quality of Billings' patriotism and the intensity of his poetic fire by reading his battle hymn:

> Let tyrants shake their iron rod,
> And slavery clank her galling chains;
> We'll fear them not, we'll trust in God.
> New England's God forever reigns.

Howe and Burgoyne and Clinton, too,
With Prescott and Cornwallis join'd
Together plot our overthrow
In one infernal league combin'd.

When God inspir'd us for the fight
Their ranks were broke, their lines were forc'd,
Their ships were shatter'd in our sight,
Or swiftly driven from our coast.

The foe comes on with haughty stride,
Our troops advance with martial noise;
Their veterans flee before our arms,
And generals yield to beardless boys.

What grateful offerings shall we bring?
What shall we render to the Lord?
Loud Hallelujahs let us sing,
And praise His name on ev'ry chord.

Billings was a many-sided man in musical
matters. He introduced the violoncello in the
church, which was a bold innovation in those days.
He also brought into use the "pitch-pipe" to deliver
choir leaders from frequent stumbling in pitching
tunes by guess work. Dr. Ritter says Billings
also originated the concert that became immensely
popular throughout New England. A writer in
the Chicago Times-Herald says Billings "paraphrased the psalms of David and brought them to
date. Appreciating the religious fervor and the
spirit of the day, he made them hymns of battle.
The people familiar with their scriptures, firm in
belief in the justice of their cause, found only

natural an application to themselves of the old
songs of bondage of the children of Israel."

It can be justly said that Billings—"the
mixture of ludicrous, eccentric, commonplace,
smart, honest, patriotic, and religious elements"—
did more for the musical advancement of New
England, considering the condition of the times
in which he lived, than any man who followed him.
For one hundred and fifty years music in New
England scarcely had a voice, until Billings came.
We are told by Hezekiah Butterworth, long connected with the Youth's Companion, that, like the
prophet of old, he led the way of those who have
made Boston a musical city. He was a man of
surprising energy. He published several books of
musical instruction, and six tune books, and nearly
all the airs were his own composition. This zealous patriot, who was the first to teach the American people to sing anthems of praise and songs of
victory, has been dead one century, lacking one
year and a half, and no monument, not so much as
a simple stone slab, marks his resting place in a
Boston graveyard.

There were many attempts to write patriotic
songs during the Revolutionary war. It seems that
almost every regiment in the colonial army had its
war poet, but when the war ended the songs were

soon forgotten. The music was "jostled out of existence" by that strangest and most grotesque of
all tunes—"Yankee Doodle." Just why the people
of that generation, and of generations since, have
accepted that tune and allowed others more meritorious to become obsolete, is a freak of the American mind that puzzles men of sober thinking. One
critic, I think it is Dr. Ritter, says that if a prize
had been offered, open to competition among all
the musicians of this globe, for the most melodi-
ously insignificant, shallow, and trivial song, the
author of "Yankee Doodle" would have received
the distinguished reward.

William Billings composed several tunes
which were worthy to continue in commemoration
of the momentous times which produced them; but
somehow—not known to our philosophy—they are
as dead as a mummy, while "Yankee Doodle," with
all its shallowness and grotesqueness, is still a pean
of victory.

Joseph Hopkinson.

IV.

The First Original American Song— "Hail Columbia."

IT is one of the curiosities of history that the first American song of a national character was written for the purpose of drawing a large house to a theatrical performance in Philadelphia in order to save a young singer and actor from pecuniary embarrassment.

Mr. S. J. Adair Fitz-Gerald, in his interesting "Stories of Famous Songs," says: "There is no romance whatever attached to the origin of 'Hail Columbia.'" It is evident that he said this because he did not understand the story of the stormy times in which this song was written.

England and France were involved in a quarrel, and war between the two countries was imminent. In 1794 the United States had concluded the Jay treaty with Great Britain, which was assailed with furious denunciations by the Republicans, who later became known as Democrats. The treaty was thought by them to be too friendly to England, as it pledged the United States not to interfere in behalf of France when a crisis was reached by the two nations. The Federalists, belonging to the administration party, gave the treaty their hearty approval, and many of them were so bitter in their hatred of France that any insult whatever from that power was enough to rouse them to advocate war. This feeling of bitterness between the Federalists and Democrats continued until 1798, when, during the height of the popular fury against France, the Federal Congress passed the famous alien and sedition acts, by which aliens were rendered liable to summary banishment from the United States at the discretion of the president. This made the breach between the factions wider than ever. Party spirit ran high. Resentfulness and hate were engendered on all hands. Mr. Motley, in his brilliant history of William the Silent, tells us that a little dog saved the Dutch Republic; and it can be said that a song, more than any other agency, incited national pride, allayed party passion, and averted a serious entanglement in the European conflict.

It was during this reign of partisanship that

a theater was opened in Philadelphia, and a benefit
was to be given to a young man, Gilbert Fox by
name, who had some talent as a singer. But the
warlike condition of things threw discouragement
on the undertaking. The singer was somewhat
acquainted with Joseph Hopkinson, who was then
a young lawyer, and calling upon him one Saturday afternoon in April, 1798, he earnestly pleaded
with him to furnish a patriotic song which could
be sung to the tune then known as the "President's
March," composed in 1789 by a German professor
in Philadelphia, named Phylo, alias Feyles, alias
Thyla, alias Phyla, alias Roth, and was first
played at Trenton when Washington was on his
way to New York to be inaugurated president.
Mr. Hopkinson's sympathy for the young man in-
duced him to write the words now recognized as
"Hail Columbia." The two stanzas which were
more frequently used than any others, are the
following:

> Hail, Columbia! happy land!
> Hail, ye heroes, heav'n born band!
>   Who fought and bled in Freedom's cause,
>   Who fought and bled in Freedom's cause,
> And when the storm of war was gone,
> Enjoyed the peace your valor won.
>   Let independence be our boast,
>   Ever mindful what it cost,
> Ever grateful for the prize,
> Let its altar reach the skies.

CHORUS:

Firm, united, let us be,
Rallying round our liberty!
As a band of brothers joined,
Peace and safety we shall find.

Immortal patriots, rise once more!
Defend your rights, defend your shore!
Let no rude foe, with impious hand,
Let no rude foe, with impious hand,
Invade the shrine where sacred lies,
Of toil and blood the well-earned prize.
While off'ring peace sincere and just,
In heaven we place a manly trust,
That truth and justice shall prevail,
And every scheme of bondage fail.

The song packed the house. It was called for
again and again during the same performance, and
at the finalé the audience rose and lustily joined
in the chorus, and the public heart was so profoundly touched by its patriotic sentiment that
England and France sank before "Hail Columbia." The song evoked such universal interest
that within a few nights after it was first given,
President Adams and the heads of all the govern-
mental departments attended the theater to hear
the new-born song, and the enthusiasm was so intense that the singer was called out time and again.

Congress was in session at the time, and when
thousands of people assembled on the streets in
the evenings, congressmen joined them in singing

the new national song. It is not a great song, perhaps, and possibly it has endured far beyond any
merit of its own, and certainly, as Judge Hopkinson says, beyond his expectation. But the song
which kindled and kept alive an American spirit,
when such a spirit was vital to national honor and
public peace—lifting the people above the disturb-
ing passions and conflicting policies of the hour—
is a song which should live always in the good will
of the American people.

V.

"The Star Spangled Banner."

OF all the songs inspired of patriotism and born in the fierce passions of war, "The Star Spangled Banner" probably has the firmest hold on the American people. It is the product of one of the most romantic and thrilling events in our national history.

With the renewal of war between England and France in 1803, came a return of trouble to the United States. Shortly after the war with France began, England claimed the right to search American vessels for deserters from the English navy. Thousands of Americans were seized and forced to fight for England; and to avenge these outrages, the United States declared war in 1812. It is another curious fact of history that the excellent frigates built during the exciting period which called forth "Hail Columbia," when the party in

Francis Scott Key.

power was thought by the opposition to be too friendly toward Great Britain, were the nucleus of the gallant navy that by and by should win such triumphs over England in the stormy times that produced "The Star Spangled Banner."

In the latter part of August, 1814, Dr. William Beanes, an old resident of Upper Marlborough, Maryland, was captured by Gen. Ross of the British army, and held as a prisoner on the admiral's flagship, the "Surprise." The doctor was a personal friend of Francis Scott Key, then a young lawyer living at Baltimore. On the 2d of September, 1814, writing from Georgetown, to his mother, Mr. Key said: "I am going to Baltimore in the morning to proceed in a flag vessel to Gen. Ross. Old Dr. Beanes, of Marlborough, is taken prisoner by the enemy, who threaten to carry him off." Key found the English fleet in Chesapeake Bay, and was kindly received by Admiral Cochrane. But the enemy was about to make a combined attack by sea and land upon Fort McHenry; and while Gen. Ross consented to the release of Dr. Beanes, it was stipulated that all of the American party should remain on the "Surprise" until the fort was reduced.

All during that eventful night, the 13th of September, the great guns of the fleet poured a

blazing shower of shot and shell upon the fortress.
Key, standing on the deck of the English ship, in
the midst of the excitement of the terrific bombardment, could see at intervals, by the glare of
the rocket and the flash of the cannon, the American flag waving victoriously over its gallant defenders. It was a hot, persistent fight, taxing the
courage, the endurance, and the patriotism of the
brave soldiers to the utmost. In the stirring enthusiasm of that supreme moment, and at the dawn's
early light, when the Stars and Stripes rose above
the smoke of conflict, and seemed to wave in
triumph from the very battlements of heaven, Key
wrote the song that should be as deathless as the
flag itself:

O say can you see by the dawn's early light,
    What so proudly we hailed at the twilight's last gleam-
        ing;
Whose stripes and bright stars thro' the perilous fight
    O'er the ramparts we watched were so gallantly stream-
        ing—
And the rocket's red glare, the bombs bursting in air,
Gave proof through the night that our flag was still there;
O say, does that star-spangled banner yet wave
O'er the land of the free and the home of the brave?

On the shore dimly seen through the mists of the deep,
    Where the foe's haughty host in dread silence reposes,
What is that which the breeze o'er the towering steep,
    As it fitfully blows, half conceals, half discloses?

Now it catches the gleam of the morning's first beam,
In full glory reflected now shines in the stream;
'Tis the star-spangled banner—Oh, long may it wave
O'er the land of the free and the home of the brave!

And where is that band who so vauntingly swore
  That the havoc of war and the battle's confusion
A home and a country should leave us no more?
  Their blood has washed out their foul footsteps' pollution.
No refuge could save the hireling and slave
From the terror of flight or the gloom of the grave;
And the star-spangled banner in triumph doth wave
O'er the land of the free and the home of the brave.

O! thus be it ever when freemen shall stand
  Between their loved homes and the war's desolation;
Blest with vict'ry and peace may the Heaven-rescued land
  Praise the Power that hath made and preserved us a
      nation.
Then conquer we must, when our cause it is just,
And this be our motto: "In God is our trust;"
And the star-spangled banner in triumph shall wave
O'er the land of the free and the home of the brave!

The day after the bombardment, Key was
taken ashore, and a clear copy of the song was
made; and the day following it was read to a
friend and kinsman of Key, Judge Nicholson,
who, delighted with it, urged that it should
be printed, and in a few hours "The Star Spangled
Banner" was read everywhere in Baltimore, and
was received with the liveliest pleasure.

How to utilize the song was the next question.
It was only a few days after the words were cir-

culated throughout the city, that a gathering of
army comrades took place at a one-story tavern
standing next door to the Holiday Street theater.
Key was present, and read the song two or three
times, and the pathetic eloquence of the lines electrified the soldiers. When some one demanded
that it should be sung, one account says that Ferdi-
nand Durang, an actor, being acquainted with an
old English air, "To Anacreon in Heaven," quickly
made the proper adaptation, and, mounting a
chair, sang the song with such voice and feeling
as to throw the hearers in the wildest state of excitement. In four days it found its way on the
stage, where it was received with spontaneous and
unbounded enthusiasm. The song seems to have
been pitched to the keynote of a screaming shell,
and everywhere, in places of amusement, in camp,
and in the home, it went straight to the popular
heart.

The old English tune, "To Anacreon in
Heaven," with which "The Star Spangled Banner"
is inseparably associated, was composed in London, sometime between 1770 and 1775, by John
Strafford Smith. He was a member of an aristo-
cratic society called the "Anacreonites," and the
regular fortnightly meetings were always opened

with the constitutional song, "To Anacreon in Heaven."

The flag of Fort McHenry, which inspired the immortal lines of "The Star Spangled Banner," was made by Mrs. Mary Pickersgill, whose mother, Rebecca Young, made the first flag carried by the colonists in the war of the Revolution. Its original dimensions were forty feet by twenty-nine, but the shells from the English fleet, and the destructiveness of time, reduced its length to thirty-two feet. It is still in a fair state of preservation, and is owned by Mr. Eben Appleton, of Yonkers, N. Y., whose grandfather, Colonel George Armstead, was one of the heroic defenders of McHenry in 1814.

Francis Scott Key was thirty-four years old when he wrote his famous song, and died on the 11th of January, 1843. William Richard Hereford sang of "Destiny" in these four lines:

"Some singers sing but a single song
And the world remembers every word,
While others sing their whole lives long,
Then die at last unknown, unheard."

Key was the singer of a single song, and his name will not fade from the minds of men as long as the Stars and Stripes endure.

There is splendid patriotism in the consecra-

tion by James Lick, of California, of $150,000
to the building and maintaining of a monument
in San Francisco dedicated to the memory of him
who wrote the first flag song of the Republic. And
the recent movement in Maryland to accept contributions of school children of that state for the
building of a monument to the memory of the
author of "The Star Spangled Banner," is a noble
expression of patriotic sentiment. We rear monuments to all sorts of heroes, and why not build
memorials of the men and women who have inspired us by their songs to win victories, not only
in war, but still greater victories in morals and
religion, and which have been won on the battle-
field of the human heart?

Colonel Henry Watterson, in his admirable ad-
dress at the unveiling of the Key monument at
Frederick, Md., on the 9th of August, 1898, said
that "the ways of Providence to man are inscrut-
able; that some mysterious power, unexplained and
unfathomable, has, from the beginning of time,
ruled the destinies of men." It is never by accident or chance that a great song that moves the
world is born. Victor Hugo tells us that it was the
decree of God—the law of the nineteenth century
—that Bonaparte should not conquer at Waterloo.
"That vast man had been impeached before the

The Key Monument, Frederick, Md.

Infinite." By an influence as divinely controlled,
Charles Wesley, an impetuous boy of fifteen, was
led to decline the heirship to the Wellesley estate
in Ireland; for, according to all human calcula-
tion, had it been otherwise, the world never would
have sung his incomparable hymns which have
touched the heart of Christendom; and the soldier
who overthrew Bonaparte—the most ambitious
despot in modern warfare—never would have been
born. Edmund Burke says: "That great chain
of causes, which, linking one to another, even to
the throne of God himself, can never be unraveled
by any industry of ours."

The hour and the man met in the struggle at
Fort McHenry, not by any power of the will or
the flesh, but by a law of the Almighty, and out of
that baptism of fire came a glorious inspiration,
and from the soul of Key burst forth "The Star
Spangled Banner," the "Gloria in Excelsis of
American freedom." It is a song that will ever
inspire a devotion to the flag, and like its companion, "Old Glory," it will never find a graveyard, but will sing on through the centuries, its
music ever accelerating the step of American freemen in the great march of human progress.

There are three national songs with which the
American people ought to be perfectly familiar—

"The Star Spangled Banner," "My Country, 'Tis of Thee," and "The Battle Hymn of the Republic." The first one chants the glory of the flag, and it is deeply to be regretted that the great mass of people are so little acquainted with the lines of the song of immortal memory. The death of that splendid and highly honored tragedian, Thomas W. Keene, which occurred in May, 1898, calls to mind the fact that a few years ago he joined several distinguished actors, singers and orators, in taking part in a Press entertainment given at Central Music Hall, Chicago. After the tremendous applause which greeted the appearance of Mr. Keene had ceased, he said he would recite something new, and began "The Star Spangled Banner." A few in the audience applauded him, others tittered, and many laughed in derision; but Mr. Keene took the outbreak pleasantly, and before proceeding further he said: " 'The Star Spangled Banner' is so new to you that I will give $100 to charity in Chicago if any man or woman in this audience will read it from memory." Not a person responded.

Whenever the spirit of patriotism rises to its divinest height, this song is sure to be present. On the Sunday following the firing on Sumter, the scene in thousands of churches in the North was one which attested the loyalty of our people; and the memory of those stirring times and all which that Sabbath meant to this Union has not grown dim in the passing of a third of a century. When men and women met to worship on that day, they also met to vow their allegiance to the flag; and in hundreds of churches the pulpits were draped with the Stars and Stripes, and there went up from the hearts, as well as from the lips of the people, the sublime strains of "The Star Spangled Banner."

Just four years after the flag was hauled down at Sumter, there was a memorable gathering at the same fort. It was on the very day Lincoln was assassinated. The self-same flag, shell-tattered in the bombardment of '61, was to be re-hoisted. Henry Ward Beecher was requested by the United States government to go to Sumter and deliver the oration. It was a day of victory for "Old Glory."

After the cannon had given some emphatic expressions of exultant gladness, the flag was uncovered at the base of the staff, and a ripple of applause passed over the multitude, but this was hushed as if by the very breath of God, and the pent-up feelings of the great orator and of the vast concourse broke out in tears and sobs of joy. But when Maj. Anderson hoisted the flag, and it floated beautifully out in the charming breeze of a perfect day, the band struck up "The Star Spangled Banner," and the people gave their patriotic emotions full sway in singing the song of the flag triumphant.

There is no other song that will stir one's patriotic blood with more vigor in any great national emergency than this anthem of the flag. One week after the blowing up of the Maine, the orchestra, at the Metropolitan Opera house in New York, had played a few bars of the regular program, when suddenly it changed to "The Star Spangled Banner." The patriotic tune had not proceeded far before there came a tremendous yell. No one knew from whence it came, for it seemed to come from everywhere at once. A report of the scene says that the patriotic play-goers forgot their surroundings, and, leaping to their feet, cheered in a way that drowned the orchestra. Women waved their fans, handkerchiefs and programs, others joined in the refrain, and finally the whole audience rose and sang the inspiring words until the music ceased; and the soul-stirring scene closed with a mighty shout that fairly shook the walls. It was said that not another such event had been witnessed in any New York theater since civil war times. It was an outburst of emotion inspired by the song, and was indicative of the state of the public mind in reference to the Cuban question. The circumstance illustrates the fact that "American patriotism is always on tap, and that the American people stand ever ready to leap, like an armed giant, into the fight at the first call of duty."

One of the most thrilling incidents in the annals of war, showing the power of patriotic song, was that on the ramparts of Santiago on that memorable Friday, the 1st of July, 1898. I think it was in the Twenty-first regulars, that man after man was fast falling in blood and death before a blazing fire of Mauser bullets, when the soldiers, catching a fresh gleam of the flag at a critical moment, spontaneously began to sing "The Star Spangled Banner," and its majestic strains so thrilled the souls of the men that they seemed to be nerved by some superhuman power to defy the storm of battle, and to win the victory that sealed the fate of Santiago.

VI

My Country, 'tis of Thee.

AMONG the mysteries of human life none is
farther beyond our power of penetration
than the inspired moment that comes to some
soul, and out of which is born a great song that
moves the heart of the world. These single flashes
of inspiration, producing songs that have so power-
fully affected the destinies of humanity, are never
repeated, in an equal degree, in the same indi-
vidual. Every poet of the soul, every minstrel of
our joys and hopes and heart-experiences, has his
masterpiece; and it seems to have been foreor-
dained that he shall never bring forth another of
like merit. There are thousands of things in these
strange lives of ours that we cannot explain, and
this is one of them. It is as great a mystery as
love, or the union of soul and body. Brander Matthews says that "no man has ever yet sat him down

Samuel F. Smith.

and taken up his pen and said, 'I will write a national hymn,' and composed either words or music which the nation was willing to take for its own." Songs that live, and make great history, are never produced in that way. When Mozart was asked how he set to work to compose a symphony, he replied: "If once you *think* how you are to do it, you will never write anything worth hearing; I write because I cannot help it."

In the making of songs many pieces "are called but few chosen." There is a single "Mount Washington" standing out in clear relief above and beyond all other songs which men and women produce. And if we turn to history we will find this illustrated in national hymns and battle songs by Francis Scott Key's "Star Spangled Banner;" Julia Ward Howe's "Battle Hymn of the Republic;" George F. Root's "Battle Cry of Freedom;" Henry C. Work's "Marching Through Georgia;" Rouget de Lisle's "Marseillaise Hymn;" Max Schenckenberger's "Watch on the Rhine;" and in sacred song by Isaac Watts' "When I Survey the Wondrous Cross;" Charles Wesley's "Jesus, Lover of My Soul;" Augustus M. Toplady's "Rock of Ages;" Edward Perronet's "All Hail the Power of Jesus' Name;" Henry Francis Lyte's "Abide With Me;" Sarah Flower Adams' "Nearer, My

God, to Thee ;" Charlotte Elliott's "Just as I Am ;"
Ray Palmer's "My Faith Looks Up to Thee ;" and
John Henry Newman's "Lead, Kindly Light."
And Dr. Samuel F. Smith was also a man of one
song—one that towers grandly above all other
songs he ever wrote. While he is the author of
that fine, popular mission hymn, "The Morning
Light Is Breaking," it was his national song that
made his name and his fame a part of the imperishable history of America and American patriotism.

Seventy years ago Dr. Smith was graduated
from Harvard University in the class with the distinguished Dr. Oliver Wendell Holmes, who, in
later years, thus referred to his classmate in a reunion poem :

> "And there's a fine youngster of excellent pith,
> Fate tried to conceal him by naming him Smith."

Three years after his graduation this
"youngster of excellent pith" wrote a poem of four
stanzas. It did not then appear to be a special con-
tribution to our patriotic literature, or of any par-
ticular value to the hymnology of the church ; but
the gift was so important—so national, so uplift-
ing, and so ennobling in its influence, that sixty-
five years later, Dr. Holmes said, a short time before his death, in 1894 : "Now, there's Smith.
His name will be honored by every school child in

the land when I have been forgotten a hundred
years. He wrote 'My Country, 'Tis of Thee.' If
he had said 'Our Country' the hymn would not
have been immortal, but that 'My' was a master-
stroke. Every one who sings the hymn at once
feels a personal ownership in his native land. The
hymn will last as long as the country."

Samuel F. Smith was born in Boston in 1808.
He became a theological student, and was graduated from Andover Seminary in 1832. The story
of the origin of the great national hymn is a simple
one and has been many times repeated. In 1832
William C. Woodbridge, a friend of Dr. Smith's,
who had been visiting Germany and the German
schools, brought home with him a lot of German
music books. Mr. Woodbridge gave the books to
Lowell Mason, who was then giving vocal music
an extraordinary impulse throughout New England; and afterwards did more to raise the standard of American church music and make it popular than any other man who ever lived. But Mr.
Mason, being unable to read German, turned the
books over to Dr. Smith, remarking at the time
that he would be pleased to have any poetical translation the young man saw proper to make. "Turn-
ing over the leaves of the books one gloomy day in
February, 1832," said Dr. Smith many years

afterwards, "I came across the air 'God Save the King.' I liked the music. I glanced at the German words at the foot of the page. Under the inspiration of the moment I went to work and in half an hour 'America' was the result. It was written on a scrap of paper I picked up from the table, and the hymn of to-day is substantially as it was written that day :"

My country! 'tis of thee,
Sweet land of liberty,
    Of thee I sing;
Land where my fathers died,
Land of the pilgrims' pride,
From every mountain side
    Let freedom ring.

My native country, thee,
Land of the noble, free,
    Thy name I love;
I love thy rocks and rills,
Thy woods and templed hills;
My heart with rapture thrills
    Like that above.

Let music swell the breeze,
And ring from all the trees
    Sweet freedom's song;
Let mortal tongues awake,
Let all that breathe partake,
Let rocks their silence break,
    The sound prolong.

Our Fathers' God, to Thee,
Author of liberty,
    To Thee we sing;
Long may our land be bright
With freedom's holy light;
Protect us by Thy might,
    Great God, our King!

Edward Everett Hale tells the pleasant story
that when he was ten years old he had spent all his
Fourth of July pennies in root-beer, ginger snaps
and oysters, at a celebration on Boston Common,
and was strolling homeward when he saw hundreds
of Sunday school children marching into Park
Street Church. Boy-like, he soon joined the pro-
cession, got into the church, made his way to the
gallery, and heard five hundred young voices sing
"My Country, 'Tis of Thee," to the tune that Dr.
Smith had found in a German music book. This
was in 1832, and was the first time the hymn had
been sung in public.

It is difficult to trace the origin of the tune
which will be forever associated with "My
Country, 'Tis of Thee." Some suppose it was
composed in England about 1715, by Henry
Carey, poet and musician, who died by his own
hand in 1743. But there seems to be no sufficient reason for attributing to him the air to which
the national hymns of America, England and

Prussia are sung. The New York Sun, in a clever answer to a correspondent as to the beginning of "America," essayed to follow the tune down the centuries as follows: "The tune was not English originally, though the English use it for their royal anthem. It was used by the Germans long before it was taken up by the English, and we are assured by a musical explorer that the Germans got it from the Norsemen, who had probably heard it sung by the Finns, who most likely captured it from the Huns, who doubtless brought it from Asia when they entered Europe. We told in the Sun long ago of our attempt to trace this very old tune through the ages, from country to country, and to its birthplace. We found that it had been known to various races, and we found it as far back as we could go. It, or something like it, was perhaps sung by the Jews in the first temple, and they may have borrowed it from the Egyptians. It is of a solemn and majestic strain, suitable to some of the Psalms of David. It is certain that the English did not invent or concoct the tune to which they sing the words of 'God Save the Queen,' and to which we sing the words of 'America.' We need not be ashamed to use the tune because it existed in other countries before we adopted it, or was used by generations that lived before Columbus discovered America, or was known to musicians before the time of St. Ambrose."

Whatever may be the history of this tune, one thing is strikingly significant: "There certainly must be something more than ordinarily inspiring in an air which has struck the popular heart of the four greatest nations of the earth."

"My Country, 'Tis of Thee" did not have a wide spread popularity until the civil war began. It was found in a few hymn books, and was sung on stated occasions, but as a national song—as a special inspirer of patriotism— it did not stir the people in any impressive degree until the flag was shot down at Sumter. Since then it has been used more frequently than any other of the so-called national songs. It is recognized the world over as a great national hymn—beautifully simple in its poetry, rich in its patriotic sentiment, and vigorous enough to reflect the ennobling spirit of true American liberty.

Dr. Smith tells us: "I have heard it on the Atlantic Ocean, on the Baltic Sea and on the Mediterranean, in London, Liverpool, Stockholm, Copenhagen, Paris, Rome, Naples, in the baths at Pompeii, in Athens, Calcutta and Rangoon. On the earth I have heard it on Pike's Peak, and under the earth in the caverns at Manitou,

Colorado, where it was played on the stalactites."
It has been sung on many a march, on battlefields,
in hospitals, on days of great rejoicing, and on days
that were dark and uncertain to those who had
sacrificed much that their country might become
indeed one "sweet land of liberty."

The song is simplicity itself, and yet it is a
curious fact that others more gifted in poetic
faculty, and of greater minds than Dr. Smith, have
tried their best to make a song which would be
truly a national anthem, but no one except this
plain, kindly and noble-hearted Baptist clergyman
has come within a thousand miles of success. He
alone has given us "My Country, 'Tis of Thee,"
and it will never be repeated.

One of the most remarkable scenes ever
witnessed on the Chicago board of trade was in
1889, when Dr. Smith, stopping in the city for a
short time, was invited to visit that famous institu-
tion. It was during business hours, and when it
became known that the author of "America" was
on 'Change, he was carried to the pit, and hundreds
of these mighty men of trade, surrounding him
with uncovered heads, began to sing "America."
It was a vast chorus of robust voices, and in the
marvelous delirium of the song the enthusiasm
knew no bounds. The intensity of the feeling

produced by the song could not be adequately described, and the scene was so singularly impressive that one writer, borrowing from Shakespeare, said:

"If I should live a thousand years
I never should forget it."

"America" is so world-wide in its fame as the national hymn of a great, liberty loving people, that a copy in Dr. Smith's own handwriting was requested by the Pope for the Vatican Library. He acceded to the papal request, and the copy was presented to his Holiness, through David Pells Secor of Bridgeport, Connecticut, on New Year's day, 1895, ten months and a half before the doctor's death.

The Kansas City Star gives an interesting little story of a tiny girl in that city who was returning home from an all-day visit somewhere, and had taken a Westport car. Her lap was full of old-fashioned flowers which she cherished with peculiar pride.

Everything was of interest to this small person, and she bobbled and squirmed about in her endeavor to miss nothing that was going on in the street or in the car. After a while she became satisfied with the life about her and settled down in quiet contentment.

She had not long been thus, and the man across
the aisle opened his paper and had forgotten her,
when she began to sing softly to herself.   At first
the man couldn't catch the tune, much less the
words.   So he pretended to be interested in his
paper.   Presently she grew bolder, or more forget-
ful of her surroundings, for in a sweet little
treble came the song, clear and bold, "My
Country, 'Tis of Thee."   She was just starting on
the verse:

> "My native country, thee,
> Land of the noble free,
>   Thy name I love;
> I love thy rocks and rills,
> Thy woods and templed hills:
> My heart with rapture thrills
>   Like that above."

Then she started on the third verse, this time a
little louder.   The men all about her dropped their
tiresome discussions of the war and business and
troubles and listened to her:

> "Let music swell the breeze,
> And ring from all the trees,
>   Sweet freedom's song."

The whole car was listening to her now.
Some men smiled, others had moist eyes, a few
slapped their knees appreciatively and muttered,
"Isn't that great?"

On she went to the end, totally oblivious to everyone. Presently talk began again, and men settled down to ordinary thoughts, but all through them rang the dear old tune of "America," and everyone felt uplifted because a little girl knew all the words of our national hymn and delighted to sing them.

It is passing strange that a national hymn, beautiful and animating in its melody and simple and inspiring in its poetry, should be so little known among the American people. Twelve or thirteen years ago, when that magnificent English steamship, the City of Berlin, then commanded by Captain Watkins, was on a return trip from Liverpool, the captain presided at an entertainment given by the passengers for the benefit of the seamen's fund. One interesting feature of the program was the singing of national songs. "God Save the Queen" was sung with wonderful power and feeling, and then Captain Watkins suggested that "America" should be sung out of courtesy to the many well-known Americans aboard. After an outburst of applause,

> "My country, 'tis of Thee,
> Sweet land of liberty,"

rose in full chorus. But at the close of the fourth line the words grew fainter and fainter, and when the end of the first verse was reached, only three voices were heard, and one of them was the gallant English captain bravely striving as best he could to sing what is called our national hymn, which the American passengers evidently could not sing.

In 1889, The Christian Union, since changed to The Outlook, said that if the patriotism of the Americans is to be measured by their familiarity with the words of our national hymn, then some other motive than "love of country" would save the nation were its freedom imperiled. It then gave the following striking incident: "On Decoration day about one hundred women were assembled in the parlors of one of the women's clubs of New York. The first number on the program was the national hymn, to be sung by the audience. The first verse was sung, after the first two lines, with firmness, the interlude was played and the first chord to begin the second verse given. There was perfect silence, except from the piano, which was under the hands of a master. Again the chord was struck, when a venturesome soul struck wildly into the first line of the third verse. Each woman gained courage and began independently wherever she chanced to remember a word, and the verse was sung in what was practically Volapük, for each mumbled the words to hide her ignorance of what the rest were singing.

Imagine that happening to a body of German women! The moment that soul-stirring 'Watch on the Rhine' was started it would roll heavenwards, in sound if not in music. The French woman would not hesitate, but boldly, firmly would sing the national hymn, living in imagination the history of her country as she sang it, while every form would respond to the command, 'To victory or death'! and an army of women would seem possible. The English woman would sing her national hymn more coldly, perhaps, but would consider herself a traitor were she not able to sing the praises of her Queen. What is the reason that an American audience stumbles and mumbles through the national hymn? The first verse can be counted as familiar, but beyond that the hymn is a failure. The intelligence of the audience has nothing to do with it. Is there not a moral force in the sentiment expressed in our hymn that would make us all feel more strongly a love of country if we could, when we come together, form a common bond of sympathy, a union of voice and heart? Every American woman should consider it her duty to know the words of our national hymn, and feel them, she should consider it a part of her duty that every child brought under her influence should know the words and understand their meaning."

The power of patriotic songs over men who have been called to march and fight, and suffer and die, for the cause of liberty and the Union, has been pathetically illustrated thousands of times. Among the Americans severely wounded in the campaign before Santiago, in the war with Spain, was Edward Marshall, the young and brilliant correspondent of The New York Journal. While lying in a hospital in New York City, where he received treatment for his wounds, he dictated an article for the September number of Scribner's Magazine, in which he gave the following picture in the field hospital at Guasimas:

"There is one incident which shines out in my memory above all others as I lie in a New York hospital writing. It was just after the battle near Santiago, on the 24th of June. It was in the field hospital, and a continual chorus of moans rose through the tree branches overhead. Amputation and death stared its members in their gloomy faces. Suddenly, a voice started softly:

'My country, 'tis of thee,
Sweet land of liberty,
Of thee I sing.'

Others then took up the lines:

'Land where my fathers died,
Land of the pilgrim's pride—'

"The quivering, quavering chorus, punctuated by groans, and made spasmodic by pain, trembled up from that little group of wounded Americans in the midst of the Cuban solitude—the pluckiest, most heartfelt song that human beings ever sang.

"But there was one voice that did not quite keep up with the others. It was so weak that it hardly could be heard until all the rest had finished with the line:

'Let freedom ring.'

"Then halting, struggling, faint, it repeated slowly:

'Land—of—the—pilgrims'—pride,
Let freedom—.'

"The last word was a woeful cry. One more son had died as died the fathers."

VII.

Columbia, the Gem of the Ocean.

A SONG of great merit, though infrequently
used compared with patriotic songs of a later
date, is "Columbia, the Gem of the Ocean."
In Mr. S. J. Adair Fitz-Gerald's "Stories of
Famous Songs," we are told that it was written
by Timothy Dwight, an ancestor of the famous
president of Yale University. How the author of
so excellent a book should drift so far from facts
in writing the story of the song, is inexplicable.
In a book published many years ago, entitled
"Airs of Many Lands," by John Philip Sousa, the
authorship of the song is given to David T. Shaw.
Mr. Sousa also adds that the music is an old English air, and the original words began, "Britannia,
the Pride of the Ocean," and that in 1852 an
American version was printed, beginning, "Columbia, the Land of the Brave." It is remarked by

musical critics that there can be no question as to the English origin of the song, for it could not possibly, they argue, have been written for America. "An island," says the doughty Bookbuyer, "might be called 'the gem of the ocean,' but the poorest poet that ever wrote would not thus designate a continent."

The authorship of the song has been in dispute for a long time, and in many of the music books the credit of writing it is given to Mr. Shaw. But a little over twenty years ago Rear-Admiral Preble, who was then preparing the first edition of "The Flag of the United States," received a letter from Mr. Thomas à Becket, which showed that the name and idea of "Columbia, the Gem of the Ocean," originated with David T. Shaw, but that the words and music, as printed and sung, were written and composed by Mr. à Becket. As the song is entitled to a permanent place among our great national hymns, it is worthy of having its history correctly written. The letter from Mr. à Becket was dated at Philadelphia, December 16, 1876, and the incidents that led up to the making of "Columbia, the Gem of the Ocean," are as follows:

"In the fall of 1843, being then engaged as an actor at the Chestnut Street Theater in this city,

I was waited upon by Mr. D. T. Shaw with the request that I would write him a song for his benefit night. He produced some patriotic lines, but I found them ungrammatical, and so deficient in measure as to be totally unfit to be adapted to music. We adjourned to the house of a friend, and I there wrote the two first verses in pencil, and composed the melody on the piano. On reaching home, I added the third verse, wrote the symphonies and arrangements, made a fair copy, and gave it to Mr. Shaw, requesting him not to sell or give a copy. A few weeks later I left for New Orleans, and was much surprised to see a published copy, entitled 'Columbia, the Gem of the Ocean,' written, composed and sung by David T. Shaw, and arranged by T. à Becket, Esq. On my return to Philadelphia, I waited upon Mr. Willig, the publisher, who told me that he had purchased the song from Mr. Shaw. I produced the original copy in pencil, and claimed the copyright, which Mr. Willig admitted. I then made arrangements with Mr. T. Osborn to publish the song in partnership; and within a week it appeared under its proper title, 'Columbia, the Gem of the Ocean,' written and composed by T. à Becket, and sung by D. T. Shaw. Mr. E. L. Davenport, the eminent actor, sang the song nightly in London for some weeks; it became very popular, and was published without authority there under the title of 'Britannia, the Gem,' etc. I visited London in 1847, and found the song claimed as an English composition. (Perhaps it is, I being an Englishman by birth.) During my absence from America, the land of my adoption, Osborn failed in business, and the plates of the song were sold to Mr. Benteen, of Baltimore. Thus it went out of my possession, much to my regret and loss."

The following is the song complete:

O Columbia, the gem of the ocean,
  The home of the brave and the free;
The shrine of each patriot's devotion
  A world offers homage to thee.
Thy mandates make heroes assemble
  When liberty's form stands in view,
Thy banners make tyranny tremble
  When borne by the red, white, and blue.
    When borne by the red, white, and blue,
    When borne by the red, white, and blue,
      Thy banners make tyranny tremble
    When borne by the red, white, and blue.

When war winged its wide desolation,
  And threaten'd the land to deform,
The ark then of freedom's foundation,
  Columbia rode safe through the storm;
With her garlands of vict'ry around her,
  When so proudly she bore her brave crew,
With her flag proudly floating before her,
  The boast of the red, white, and blue.

The boast of the red, white, and blue,
The boast of the red, white, and blue,
    With her flag proudly floating before her,
The boast of the red, white, and blue.

The wine cup, the wine cup, bring hither,
    And fill you it true to the brim,
May the wreaths they have won never wither,
    Nor the star of their glory grow dim.
May the service united ne'er sever,
    But they to their colors prove true,
The army and navy forever,
    Three cheers for the red, white, and blue.
        Three cheers for the red, white, and blue,
        Three cheers for the red, white, and blue,
            The army and navy forever,
    Three cheers for the red, white, and blue.

John Brown.

VIII

The Fatherless Song of John Brown's Body.

WHEN the flag was shot down at Sumter the whole country quivered with new emotion. As I have already said, the feeling of great numbers always tends to utterance in song. The people of the North wanted to sing, but there was no national anthem which seemed to fit the occasion. The great theme of the war called for a new song, one which would strike a chord that had not yet been touched. The time had come for fresh lyrics, for a new, generation of men—some outburst of a fiery, patriotic sentiment which would quickly take deep root in the hearts of the people. No sooner, therefore, had the belching guns at Sumter proclaimed that civil war was our misfortune, than there came into being, as if by magic and inspiration, a new, strange song, with its weird but enchanting chorus, an outburst of the genius of the nation—the song that kept in unison with the steady tramp of the armies on their way to fields of battle.

The John Brown song has been called a "spontaneous generation of the uprising of the North," the refrain of which became the marching song of the Union in the very earliest months of the war. When the war cloud had overshadowed the loyal states, there was started in Boston harbor, as if it were a bold and defiant reply to the Confederate guns at Charleston, the song of "John Brown's Body;" and the almost religious enthusiasm of the words so blended with the exciting tread of the music, as to make it an irresistible force in arousing a spirit of patriotism among the soldiers. It has a grim, uncouth melody, and a commanding refrain created, somehow, to enshrine the faith of the loyal states and the beneficence to humanity of the great civil war. The late Richard Henry Dana, Jr., author of that famous little book, "Two Years Before the Mast," writing of this nondescript, fatherless song, said: "It would have been past belief had we been told that the almost undistinguishable name of John Brown should be whispered among four millions of slaves and sung wherever the English language is spoken, and incorporated into an anthem to whose solemn cadences men would march to battle by tens of thousands."

It is a curious fact that a war song so gifted with power for victory as that of "John Brown's Body," should have an origin so disputed and involved. Its beginning may not extend into dim antiquity, like the story of "Yankee Doodle," but there is so much of the unknown about both words and music, that historians have been extremely perplexed in the effort to give the public facts, rather than legend and fiction, as to the origin of the song. Some writers—and there are no visible reasons why their story is not as believable as that of anybody else—claim that the music was adapted and the words paraphrased from an old Methodist camp-meeting hymn, which drew its form and tune in turn from a domestic ballad of a thousand years ago, just as Luther, or, more properly, William Franck, found "Old Hundred" in the ancient and simple home music of the peasantry.

Some twenty-five years ago there was a long discussion in the New York and Boston papers as to who should be credited with the authorship of this famous song of the Rebellion. But the voluminous correspondence did not disentangle history from theory and speculation.

When the Twelfth Massachusetts infantry—
commanded by Colonel Fletcher Webster, son of
Daniel Webster—was stationed at Fort Warren,
in Boston harbor, in the spring of 1861, a quartette
belonging to the Second battalion amused themselves by singing:

> "John Brown's body lies mouldering in the grave.
> His soul is marching on.
> Glory, glory, hallelujah,
> His soul is marching on."

This was the only stanza known when the quartette introduced the song at Fort Warren. In a
few weeks it developed into the following:

> "John Brown's body lies a-mouldering in the grave,
> John Brown's body lies a-mouldering in the grave,
> John Brown's body lies a-mouldering in the grave,
> His soul is marching on.
> Glory, glory, hallelujah!
> Glory, glory, hallelujah!
> Glory, glory, hallelujah!
> His soul is marching on,"

which was adopted by the army and became the
first stanza of the great war song which has been
many times heard around the world. The words
have been attributed to Mr. Charles S. Hall, of
Charlestown, Mass., and in a letter to The Boston
Transcript, in 1874, he claims to have written
most of the stanzas. Mr. Hall also says that the
music set to the words was found by Mr. James

E. Greenleaf, of Charlestown, in the archives of the church to which he was organist. The words of which Mr. Hall is said to be the author, and which constitute the original John Brown song, and adopted by the Grand Army of the Republic, are as follows:

John Brown's body lies a mould'ring in the grave,
John Brown's body lies a mould'ring in the grave,
John Brown's body lies a mould'ring in the grave,
 His soul is marching on!
 Glory, glory, hallelujah!
 Glory, glory, hallelujah!
 Glory, glory, hallelujah!
 His soul is marching on.

The stars of heaven are looking kindly down,
The stars of heaven are looking kindly down,
The stars of heaven are looking kindly down,
 On the grave of old John Brown!
 Glory, glory, hallelujah, etc.

He's gone to be a soldier in the army of the Lord.
He's gone to be a soldier in the army of the Lord,
He's gone to be a soldier in the army of the Lord!
 His soul is marching on!
 Glory, glory, hallelujah, etc.

John Brown's knapsack is strapped upon his back,
John Brown's knapsack is strapped upon his back,
John Brown's knapsack is strapped upon his back!
 His soul is marching on!
 Glory, glory, hallelujah, etc.

The tune was wonderfully catching, and as Brander Matthews has said in The Century, there

was no lack of poets to furnish words for the
music. Henry Howard Brownell, the gifted poet
of the civil war—the warm friend of Admiral Far-
ragut and Oliver Wendell Holmes—soon after
the war broke out, wrote a poem of five stanzas,
and called it, "Words That Can Be Sung to the
'Hallelujah Chorus,' " the first of which was:

"Old John Brown lies a-mould'ring in the grave,
Old John Brown lies slumbering in his grave—
But John Brown's soul is marching with the brave,
     His soul is marching on.
Glory, glory, hallelujah!
Glory, glory, hallelujah!
Glory, glory, hallelujah!
     His soul is marching on."

The remaining stanzas were so irregular in
meter that they could not be sung to the John
Brown tune without considerable patchwork, and
the poem, though in many respects meritorious,
was never adopted by the people.

A far better poem—fine in sentiment, perfect
in meter, and smooth in rhythm—is that written
by Miss Edna D. Proctor. With the exception of
Julia Ward Howe's "Battle Hymn of the Republic," of which I shall speak at length further on,
it is the best poem ever adapted to the John Brown
air. It was written shortly after Sumter fell, and
why it did not become the song of the people,

rather than the words attributed to Mr. Hall, is a psychological problem difficult to solve. The words are so worthy of being repeated that I give them in full:

John Brown died on the scaffold for the slave;
Dark was the hour when we dug his hallowed grave;
Now God avenges the life he gladly gave,
    Freedom reigns to-day!
    Glory, glory, hallelujah!
    Glory, glory, hallelujah!
    Glory, glory, hallelujah!
    Freedom reigns to-day!

John Brown sowed, and the harvesters are we;
Honor to him who has made the bondmen free;
Loved evermore shall our noble ruler be,
    Freedom reigns to-day!

John Brown's body lies mouldering in the grave;
Bright o'er the sod let the starry banner wave;
Lo! for the million he periled all to save,
    Freedom reigns to-day!

John Brown's soul through the world is marching on;
Hail to the hour when oppression shall be gone;
All men will sing in the better day's dawn,
    Freedom reigns to-day!

John Brown dwells where the battle strife is o'er;
Hate cannot harm him, nor sorrow stir him more;
Earth will remember the martyrdom he bore,
    Freedom reigns to-day!

John Brown's body lies mouldering in the grave;
John Brown lives in the triumph of the brave;
John Brown's soul not a higher joy can crave,
    Freedom reigns to-day!

As to the origin of the tune, there is a story told that in 1856, one William Steffe, of Philadelphia, who had somewhat of a local reputation as a composer of light music, was requested to furnish a fire company at Charleston, S. C., an air to some words, the chorus of which began—

"Say, bummers, will you meet us?"

In response to the wishes of the firemen, Mr. Steffe composed the tune now known as "John Brown." The happy mingling of the words and music made the song very popular, and finally the tune was taken up by the Young Men's Christian Association in the East, and set to the words well known forty years ago—

"Say, brothers, will you meet us,
Say, brothers, will you meet us,
Say, brothers, will you meet us,
    On Canaan's happy shore?
By the grace of God we'll meet you,
By the grace of God we'll meet you,
By the grace of God we'll meet you,
    Where parting is no more."

This hymn is found in the supplement to The Plymouth Collection, compiled by Henry Ward Beecher, and printed at some period between 1855 and 1860; and a correspondent in The Boston Journal, in 1874, says the tune, with only a few changes, was used by the Millerites in 1843 to the words—

"We'll see the angels coming
Through the old church yards,
Shouting through the air
Glory, glory, hallelujah."

It seems that the tune was quite well known among the negroes of the South during the civil war. Lieutenant Chandler, writing on Sherman's march to the sea, says that when a halt was made at Shady Dale, in Georgia, the band struck up "John Brown's Body," when, to the amusement and surprise of the soldiers, a number of negro girls came out from the houses, which were supposed to be deserted, and, forming in a circle around the band, danced in perfect time, and in a grave and dignified manner, as if influenced by some magical or religious ceremony. When the tune had ceased, the girls quietly returned to their cabins without a smile on their faces to disturb the gravity of their deportment; and no other tune the band might play could induce them to dance. It was learned from the older negroes that the air was known among them as the "wedding tune," that it had no connection with any hymn or song, and that the colored girls were taught that they must dance whenever they heard it played, or they

would never be married. It is not improbable
that it is one of those strange voodoo airs, so mysterious in their origin as to baffle historians.

There is abundant evidence to prove that the
tune of "John Brown" was known in Boston some
time before it was sung at Fort Warren. The most
significant event just before the outbreak of the
Rebellion, one which sent a wave of excitement
over the entire North, was the hanging of John
Brown on the 2d of December, 1859. The feeling
which that execution roused in Massachusetts
found relief in a monstrous mass meeting held at
Faneuil hall. John A. Andrew, a man whose phil-
anthropy and loyalty will long enrich the pages
of American history, was at the time governor of
the state. He took a deep interest in that memorable meeting, and on that night vast crowds of
young men and boys marched through the streets
of Boston, singing, in contempt of the governor
and of the great gathering, the improvised words
to the "John Brown" air—

> "Tell John Andrew that John Brown is dead,
> Tell John Andrew that John Brown is dead,
> Tell John Andrew that John Brown is dead,
>   And salt won't save him now."

The "John Brown" song as used in the army
was first sung by Webster's famous regiment in

Boston on the 18th of July, 1861, with one thousand and forty voices on the chorus. The occasion was the presentation of a flag to the regiment
by the Hon. Edward Everett. A few days later
the Twelfth started for the front, and on its way
electrified New York with the song; three days
afterwards it startled Baltimore; and another example of the terrible sarcasm of fate was witnessed
when the regiment, on the 1st of March, 1862,
formed a hollow square around the very spot on
which John Brown was executed at Charlestown,
Va., and these "Websters" sang with a power and
feeling never heard before—

> "John Brown's body lies a-mouldering in the grave,
>   His soul is marching on."

The Twelfth Massachusetts, commanded by
Colonel Webster, had made the song of "John
Brown" popular in the army. They always sang
it with mighty unction. The colonel was killed
in the second battle of Bull Run, August 30, 1862,
and there is pathos in the story that after the
tragedy of that day the regiment never again sang
of "Old John Brown." In July, 1864, the term
of enlistment expired, and the Twelfth returned
to Boston. It left the city three years before with
a numerical strength of one thousand and forty,

but the waste of disease, and the shot and shell of
many battles made frightful mortality among the
men ; and the sad remnant of the once famous regiment made the homeward march through the
streets of Boston with only eighty-five men. The
colors were tattered, the boys stood in mournful
evidence of hard service, and while they received
a royal welcome by a vast, patriotic multitude, and
shout after shout went up for "John Brown's
Body," these brave heroes, silently, but with a sol-
dierly tread, marched to the barracks, and the
"Websters," having finished their work, "passed
into history."

Mr. Brander Matthews is authority for the
story that after the performance of that great
chorus, "Glory to God on High," from Mozart's
Twelfth Mass, on the first day of the Boston Peace
Jubilee, an old soldier of the Webster regiment
took occasion to shake hands with Mr. Gilmore,
and to tender his congratulations on the success of
the undertaking, remarking that for his part what
he liked best was the piece called the "Twelfth
Massachusetts."

The song of "John Brown's Body" was indeed
a blast of triumph. The massive simplicity of the
tune stirred the blood of the people like a blare of
a trumpet. When Webster's regiment marched

down Broadway, New York, July 24, 1861, on their way to battle and victory, singing "Old John Brown" as a marching song, the scene was soul-stirring surpassing description. The effect was supreme. All over the North, in all Federal camps, the refrain, with its "majestic plainness in the rhythm like the beating of mighty hammers," spread as if by enchantment, and it became the battle-cry of hundreds of thousands and the Marseillaise of Emancipation.

Many songs may come and go with the occasions that produce them, but "Old John Brown" will remain. Travelers say that they have heard it among the common people of almost every clime on earth, in regions where newspapers never go, and where the story of John Brown's martyrdom could find its way only by some sort of special providence. It is not a meritorious song in point of construction, but it is strangely effective, and the explanation is that back of the song lies the sublime truth that the man whom it celebrates died for men, and immortalized his name by performing, as he saw it, a service for human liberty. "His soul is marching on." "In that solemn and significant refrain is the whole story; and it is a story that touches the human heart wherever there is love of right, of justice and of goodness."

The song has been a marvelous inspiration, and among the many thrilling experiences with which it has been associated, none has been more striking than that related by Admiral Schley in describing the destruction of Cervera's fleet off Santiago, on Sunday, July 3, 1898. Speaking of the men behind the guns, "those noble, silent, effective workers"—the firemen and coal-heavers—he tells of their singing "John Brown's Body" with wonderful meaning as they shoveled coal in the great furnaces that carried the flagship Brooklyn to such a splendid victory.

John Habberton, the author of that popular book, "Helen's Babies"—"embracing the record for a single day of the doings of a brace of boys of whom the author is half owner"—gives his impression of this song: "It has wonderful influence over me. I heard it in western camp meetings and negro cabins when I was a boy, and saw the Twelfth Massachusetts march down Broadway, singing the same air during a rush to the front in the early days of the war. I heard it sung by warrior tongues in nearly every Southern state; my old brigade sung it softly, but with a swing that was terrible in its earnestness, as they lay behind their stacks of arms, just before going into action. I have heard it played over the graves of many a dead comrade, the semi-mutinous—the cavalry became peaceful and patriotic again as their bandmaster played the old air, after having asked permission to try his hand on them ; it is the tune that burst forth spontaneously in our barracks on that glorious morning when we learned that the war was over, and it was sung with words adapted to the occasion by some rebel friends of mine on our first social meeting after the war."

On the 16th of November, 1864, General Sherman's magnificent army of 55,300 men began the famous march from Atlanta to the sea. Behind this splendidly organized army, which had won so many brilliant victories, lay Atlanta, "smouldering and in ruins, the black smoke rising high in the air and hanging like a pall over the ill-fated city." When the Fourteenth corps, on the right of the left wing, moved quickly in the grand column, one of the bands struck up "John Brown's Body." The men caught up the refrain—"Glory, glory, hallelujah,"—and it is doubtful if at any other time during the civil war, or on any occasion since, the simple but significant words were sung with bolder spirit or with mightier meaning than on the beginning of the march that has been immortalized in song and story. General Sherman afterwards said that the incident was one of the most remarkable illustrations of the influence of song he had ever known.

This, in part, is the story of one of the most mystical songs of any country or age. Why "the undistinguishable name of John Brown should have been whispered by four million slaves, and sung wherever the English language is spoken, or incorporated into an anthem" which thrilled great armies with delight and inspiration, will remain in the realm of mystery.

RESTO CHI.

George F. Root.

IX.

George F. Root and His Battle Cry of Freedom.

IT is to the honor of this sweet land of liberty
that it has reared up men adequate to every
crisis, however great. When a soldier was
needed to fight a trying war, and a statesman to lay
the foundation of a Republic, Washington—the
imperial character—heeded the stern voice of duty
and wrested victory from the most powerful nation
on earth.

When America called for orators to defend the
constitution and plead the cause of human liberty,
there rang out the clarion-like voices of Webster,
Clay, Wendell Phillips, Garfield and Beecher.

When rebellion threatened the life of the nation and the political sky was red with passion,
and a patriot and a genius was wanted to lead a
brave people through the storm of war and clouds
of uncertainty, a product of hardship and toil at

once stood before the gaze of the civilized world— a man ever righteous in purpose, amazing in wisdom, glorious in his human-ness of nature, sublime in his faith in men—Lincoln, the loftiest type of American civilization.

When the call went forth for men to save the country and its flag, in quick response came the sturdy warrior Sherman, and the fighting Sheridan; and there came from poverty and obscurity, a man of indomitable energy, silent in words, but marvelous in execution, supreme in every supreme moment, as modest as a maiden but greater than the Cæsars—General Grant, who, measured by what he did, was the greatest commander that ever led an army to victory.

When the grand army of volunteers rallied for liberty and the Union, and the homes of the people and the boys in battle called for songs of hope which should make every chord of the soul vibrate and give promise of victory, among Fortune's best gifts were George F. Root, Henry C. Work, and Julia Ward Howe—the great patriotic singers of the century.

There has never been an emergency without a man or woman to meet it. And it has been said that "God chooses His own instruments for the development of the Divine problem, and while men

may come and go, and try and fail, the right man
to perform the right service is always certain to
appear at the right time." This truth has been
demonstrated in every trying crisis in our national
history from Washington in the Revolution to
McKinley at the White House, Dewey at Manila and Schley at Santiago. And when President
Lincoln issued his second call for troops in the
summer of 1861, the emergency had come when
the Union army needed a battle cry of freedom,
and George F. Root, living in Chicago, was deeply
impressed with the mighty significance of the proclamation, and one afternoon he caught the spirit
of the hour and there began to evolve in his mind
the sentiment of a rallying song, and in an outburst of patriotic fervor there came the words and
music of that soul-stirring and pulse-quickening
battle hymn:

> Yes, we'll rally round the flag, boys,
>   We'll rally once again,
> Shouting the battle cry of freedom.
> We will rally from the hillside,
>   We will rally from the plain,
> Shouting the battle cry of freedom.
>
> CHORUS.
> The Union forever! Hurrah, boys, hurrah!
> Down with the traitors, up with the stars,
>   While we rally round the flag, boys,
>   Rally once again,
> Shouting the battle cry of freedom.

We are springing to the call
  Of our brothers gone before,
Shouting the battle cry of freedom,
And we'll fill the vacant ranks
  With a million freemen more,
Shouting the battle cry of freedom.

We will welcome to our numbers
  The loyal, true and brave,
Shouting the battle cry of freedom,
And altho' they may be poor,
  Not a man shall be a slave,
Shouting the battle cry of freedom.

So we're springing to the call
  From the East and from the West,
Shouting the battle cry of freedom,
And we'll hurl the rebel crew
  From the land we love the best,
Shouting the battle cry of freedom.

The next evening, says Mr. Root in his interesting "Story of a Musical Life," the famous Lumbard brothers—Jules and Frank, the great singers of the war—were to sing at a meeting to be held in the Chicago Court House square. Mr. Root gave them the "Battle Cry of Freedom." The magnificent voices of the brothers were electrifying; and in trumpet-like tones the refrain—

"The Union forever! Hurrah, boys, hurrah!"

spread as if impelled by some magnetic influence, and almost instantly the grand chorus rose in mighty music from the vast multitude. The song struck fire, and leaped into widespread popularity and usefulness. Only a few days after the song was written a monstrous war-meeting was held in Union Square, New York. The excitement ran high, and the emotion was intense. The Hutchinson family sang the "Battle Cry of Freedom." The immense throng of listeners were aroused to the highest pitch of exaltation of soul. The song was sung again and again, and the great audience caught up the refrain, and it proved a resistless force in swelling the ranks of the army. No other war song was sung with bolder patriotism or with a more triumphant passion of the soul. It seemed to mount up as if on the wings of magic, and was carried over all the North, and into all camps where the Stars and Stripes floated. It was often ordered to be sung as the men marched into action; and more than once its strains rose on the battle-field to stimulate courage.

There is a stirring illustration of how this song saved a battle, which I find in Brainard's "Our War Songs, North and South." During the terrible battle of the Wilderness on the 6th of May, 1864, a brigade of the Ninth Army Corps, having broken the enemy's line by an assault, became exposed to a flank attack, and with heavy loss were driven back in disorder. They retreated but a

few hundred yards, however, when they re-formed,
and again confronted the enemy. Just then some
gallant fellow—an unknown hero—in the Forty-
fifth Pennsylvania, with a head filled with sense
and a heart full of courage and song, began to sing:

"We'll rally round the flag, boys,
    Rally once again,
Shouting the battle cry of freedom."

The refrain was caught up by the entire regiment, and also by the regiments next in line. The
air was filled with the crackle and smoke of the
burning underbrush; the pitiful cries of the
wounded, the rattle of musketry, and the wild
shouts of command, gave intense excitement to the
scene; but above all, answering the exalted yell of
the enemy, rose supreme the inspiring chorus—

"The Union forever! Hurrah, boys, hurrah!
Down with the traitors, up with the stars,
    And we'll rally round the flag, boys,
        Rally once again,
    Shouting the battle cry of freedom."

What an impressive example of the power of
patriotic song in evoking from men, when charg-
ing in the very jaws of death, a resolute and a singing spirit!

There is an influence beautiful and marvelous
in these songs of soul and war. Dr. H. H. Bel-
field, formerly adjutant of a regiment of Iowa

cavalry, and afterwards principal of the Chicago
Manual Training School, relates an incident in
Dr. Root's "Story of a Musical Life," which,
briefly told, is that on the last day of July, in 1864,
some of our prisoners of war were taken to Newman, Ga. The flag under which they had been
fighting had gone down in blood and death. The
Confederate flag was flying in temporary triumph
over this small company of Union soldiers who,
having obeyed orders they well knew would sacri-
fice themselves, had saved hundreds of their
comrades, and now were prisoners of war. They
were hungry, ragged, tired out, defeated, but full
of hope and song. When the inhabitants of the
town gathered about this little band of prisoners,
curious to know what the Yankee soldier looked
like, the brave, patriotic boys sang "Rally Round
the Flag." It might seem foolhardy to rouse the
Confederate town with such song, but the people
received it kindly, however, and called for more
songs; but the poor fellows had had no food for a
whole day and begged for something to eat. Food
was brought them, and the prisoners repaid the
kindness by singing more of the battle songs of
the Union, which finally found expression in
cheers of good will.

Only those who were at the front, marching

and battling for the flag and enduring all the hardships of an active army life and entering into all the painful uncertainties of war, can fully realize how often the soldiers were cheered and inspired by the words and tunes of patriotic zeal.

In the battle of Nashville a soldier was severely wounded, and in the hospital, when he had come from under the influence of chloroform, he felt that his right arm was gone. He asked that it be brought to him that he might see it once more. Taking the cold fingers in his left hand, he said, "Good-bye, old arm; we have been a long time together; we must now part. You will never fire another carbine or swing another saber for the government. Good-bye." Great tears rolled down his cheeks as the shattered arm was taken from his sight. He called for one of the songs of the Union, and inspired by the music of patriotism, he said, "Don't misunderstand me, doctor; I don't regret the arm is lost. I would rather have it torn from my body than that a single star should be taken from the flag."

I do not think that we shall know, this side of eternity, how important the helpfulness and how enduring the influence of these songs of war were. A few years ago in a story, that has now become quite familiar, written by Richard W. Browne for

The Century Magazine, he says that shortly after
Lee's surrender, a number of Union officers
assembled in Richmond one evening and sang some
favorite college songs. Directly across the street
was a house occupied by some Confederate officers,
and being so near by, the Union men deemed it
improper to sing army songs, as they did not wish
to lacerate the feelings of a fallen foe. But after
several beautiful college pieces had been sung, the
lady of the house where the Federals were stopping, handed one of them a note which came from
the Confederate officers. It was a gracious request
that permission might be granted them to go over
and hear the Union men sing. Of course, consent
was gladly given, and the boys again sang some of
their glee songs. But one of the Confederate officers said in a kind tone: "Gentlemen, you sing
delightfully; but what we want to hear now are
some of your army songs." Then they sang with
force and zeal, "Marching Through Georgia,"
"John Brown's Body," "Tramp, Tramp, Tramp,
the Boys Are Marching," "Rally Round the Flag,"
and finally "The Star Spangled Banner." And
even some of the Confederate feet were inspired
to beat time to these grand songs, as if they had
never stepped to any but the "music of the Union."

After the applause had subsided, one of the

Confederate officers exclaimed, "I tell you, gentlemen, if we'd had your songs, we'd have whipped
you out of your boots. Who couldn't have marched
and fought with such songs as yours? We had
nothing but a bastard 'Marseillaise,' 'Bonny Blue
Flag,' 'Dixie,' which are nothing but jigs, and
'Maryland, My Maryland,' the tune of which is
no more inspiring than the 'Dead March in Saul,'
while your Yankee songs are full of marching and
fighting."

There is great force in the remark of the Confederate officer as to the marching and fighting
power of the "Yankee" war songs. The songs of
the Union were songs of unquenchable patriotism;
and evoked all the noble emotions in the soldier
and kept alive the spirit of mirth and hope.

The best natured soldiers on earth are those
who march under the folds of "Old Glory." Mr.
Brander Matthews, in The Century Magazine,
says the Federal soldiers never allowed pleasant
humor to desert him; and in the hard tussle of the
civil war, when roads were muddy, marching
heavy, and the hardtack scarce, and tough enough
to be marked B. C., how often the gentle lines of
"Mary Had a Little Lamb" were snugly fitted to
the tune of the "Battle cry of freedom," and many
a regiment shortened a weary march, or made a
dull camp gladsome by singing—

"Mary had a little lamb,
   Its fleece was white as snow,
   Shouting the battle cry of freedom;
And everywhere that Mary went,
   The lamb was sure to go,
   Shouting the battle cry of freedom."

As a piece of poetry, the "Battle Cry of Freedom" may not have great merit, but as an expression of patriotism it is beyond all price. It is great enough to gain enduring fame as a battle song; great enough for volunteers to sing on their marches from home in defense of the Union; great enough to be on their lips on going into battle; great enough to be associated with all the fierce struggles of the civil war; and great enough to be sung by ten thousand manly voices in a national convention that it might rouse enthusiasm for the peerless soldier of history.

The late Charles A. Dana, editor of The New York Sun, and Assistant secretary of war during the Rebellion, said, a short time before his death, in October, 1897, that Dr. Root did more to preserve the Union than a great many brigadier-generals, and quite as much as some brigades. The editor of The Musical Visitor, Mr. Murray, says he heard the "Battle Cry of Freedom" sung in the outer line of intrenchments before Petersburg, within talking distance of the Confederate line of battle, the men voicing the lines of the song with remarkable enthusiasm when they knew full well that the very next minute "they might have to give their lives for the Union they were fighting to maintain."

Among many incidents connected with Dr. Root's war songs, the one which touched him most deeply is related in his delightful "Story of a Musical Life." An Iowa regiment went in one of the charges during the siege of Vicksburg eight hundred strong, and came out with a terrible loss of more than half their number. But the remnant of the regiment left the battlefield waving their torn and powder-stained flag singing—

"Yes, we'll rally round the flag, boys."

Years after the war, the doctor held a musical convention in Anamosa, Iowa, and one evening he received a note, saying, "If the author of the 'Battle Cry of Freedom' would sing that song it would gratify many soldiers in the audience who used to sing it in the army." Before singing the song, Dr. Root related an incident of the charge of the Iowa regiment, when some one shouted, "Here is a soldier who lost an arm in that charge." And at the doctor's request the veteran went forward and stood upon the platform while the song was being sung. He was a tall, fine-looking man, and the mournful eloquence of the empty sleeve, and the soul-thrilling lines of the "Battle Cry of Freedom" as sung by Dr. Root, brought tears to the eyes of almost the entire audience.

Dr. Root was born in Sheffield, Mass., in 1820. He came into the world with music in his soul. The dream of his life was to be a musician. In 1858 he started a music business in Chicago. He had composed that beautiful tune, "Shining Shore," and several other well known tunes and anthems prior to that time. His first war song was the "Battle Cry of Freedom," the authorship of which is fame enough for any one man. He died August 7, 1895.

Dr. Root played an important part in the war for the Union. His songs were a great force in the homes as well as in the field. They were the most eloquent appeals for enlistments. They touched the chords of patriotism as they had never been touched before. They became the ruling sentiment of the American people, and millions rallied round the flag. Dr. Root had a greater influence during the dark days of the war than many men who happened to have their names written among immortal heroes. His influence through his songs was immeasurable in a special time of need, and will still live, and while coming generations "will not forget the song," they cannot forget the singer.

On the afternoon of July 4, 1896, a vast audience of ten thousand assembled at the Coliseum in Chicago, the occasion being a war song festival for the benefit of the George F. Root monument fund. It was a great day for the "Battle Cry of Freedom." Chicago's greatest singers took the solos, and one thousand children sang in the choruses. Mr. Jules Lumbard, the white-haired veteran, who was first to sing that famous battle hymn thirty-five years before, sang it at the Coliseum, and every soul was thrilled by its new-born power. Luther Laflin Mills, that superb orator, delivered the oration, and one quotation therefrom will close this chapter on the "Battle Cry of Freedom:"

"The story of the war songs of Root is the story of the songs of every people. Cradle songs become crystallized in human character; home songs running through the memories of men are the thread of gold which binds them to purity, and sacred hymns once learned in childhood, and arousing the dullest ear in after years, are a constant link between God and man. Songs are easy sermons. Their power abides. The songs of George F. Root

Jules Lumbard,
THE FIRST SINGER OF "THE BATTLE CRY OF FREEDOM"

abide, and will remain in the memories and voices of our people, not only as reminders of the nation's heroic struggle for self-preservation, but as a constant, inspiring and educating force in maintaining and strengthening the lofty sentiment of American patriotism."

X.

Tbe Battle Hymn of tbe Republic.

WHEN the civil war broke out there was no great national hymn, generally accepted as such. It is safe to say that not one in a thousand could sing from memory either "The Star Spangled Banner," or that ever beautiful and always inspiring, patriotic hymn, "America." For years the people had been discrediting our patriotic songs by neglecting to study them; and to-day newspapers and periodicals are disputing over the question whether or no we really have an appropriate national hymn; and the effort to form a common bond of sympathy or fellowship by the union of heart and voice on memorized patriotic songs is usually a dismal failure.

Some nine or ten years ago there was a reunion of hundreds of students in Paris that included representatives from many countries. One excellent

Julia Ward Howe.

feature of the program was the singing of favorite
national songs by the respective nationalities. The
Russians, Swiss, Germans, English, French and
Italians sang their songs in splendid chorus, but
when the young Americans were called upon to
respond with one or two popular national songs,
they were at a loss what to do, for not one of them
could start a single American patriotic song.
Finally a happy thought struck the students from
the Southern states, and they sang, as best they
could, "We'll Hang John Brown," and the Northern boys, who were in the majority, followed with
the old army song, "We'll Hang Jeff Davis to a
Sour Apple Tree;" and the first feeling of mortifi-
cation was dispelled by the uproarious merriment
that followed.

William E. Curtis, the Washington correspondent of The Chicago Record, tells the story
that ex-Senator John Sherman pays so little atten-
tion to our national songs that he hardly knows
one from another. During the presidential campaign of 1896, while he was stumping in Ohio, the
band played "I'm Looking for the Bully of the
Town" to open his meeting. As soon as it finished
that spirited air Mr. Sherman arose and declared
that nothing so inspired a citizen with patriotism
for the performance of his duties to his country

as the majestic strains of our grand old national
hymn, "The Star Spangled Banner," and he
thanked the band for giving him the text for his
speech. Everybody laughed, of course, and Mr.
Sherman said afterwards that it was the most
irreverent audience he had ever addressed.

This need of a new national hymn to meet new
and exciting conditions, one that would be the
great peace song, yet the war song of the nation—
the national heart-beat set to music—was deeply
felt at the very beginning of the civil war. At the
request of many prominent Union men, a committee, composed of scholars and statesmen, among
whom were George William Curtis, Hamilton
Fish, and General John A. Dix, was appointed to
select such a hymn for the use of the homes in the
North and the army in the field. The committee
waited three months for such a song. Twelve hundred competitors presented their compositions for
the prize of $250 for the words and $250 for the
music; but not one of them was accepted. The
committee found that there was no soul-feeling, no
fire of patriotism, running through any of the
songs. It is just as possible to run a steam engine
with ice water as to produce a great song without
inspiration. Some one has said that money may
buy machinery—sometimes in the form of men—

but inspiration, never. Once Robert Collyer nestled up to the side of Samuel F. Smith and quietly asked him how he wrote "My Country, 'tis of Thee," and the venerable doctor answered, "It was not written—it just came." 'Great songs, whether patriotic or religious, flow from hearts beating with noble emotion; and of all the twelve hundred songs composed in 1861 in competition for the prize of $500, not one is alive to-day.

'But Julia Ward Howe, then not widely known as a poet, had visited the army of the Potomac, and there she saw the commotion of war, the bodies shattered, the lives sacrificed, and the stress and agony of the government in its mortal grapple with rebellion. These things lay heavy upon her heart, which throbbed in unison with the great heart of the nation; and one night in December, in 1861, she sprang from her bed and wrote the expression of her soul in these words of living power:

Mine eyes have seen the glory of the coming of the Lord;
He is trampling out the vintage where the grapes of wrath
    are stored;
He hath loosed the fateful lightning of his terrible, swift
    sword:
            His truth is marching on.

I have seen him in the watch-fires of a hundred circling
    camps;
They have builded him an altar in the evening dews and
    damps;

1 can read his righteous sentence by the dim and flaring
    lamps:
        His day is marching on.

1 have read a fiery gospel, writ in burnished rows of steel;
"As ye deal with my contemners, so with you my grace shall
    deal;
Let the hero, born of woman, crush the serpent with his heel,
        Since God is marching on."

He has sounded forth the trumpet that shall never call
    retreat;
He is sifting out the hearts of men before his judgment
    seat;
Oh, be swift, my soul, to answer him! be jubilant, my feet!
        Our God is marching on.

In the beauty of the lilies Christ was born across the sea,
With a glory in his bosom that transfigures you and me;
As he died to make men holy, let us die to make men free,
        While God is marching on.

The hymn reads like an inspiration, and it is
no wonder that it is known wherever the English
language is spoken. The music made the words
of "John Brown's Body" famous, but Mrs. Howe's
matchless battle song has made the melody
immortal.

The story of the writing of the song has been
told many times, but for the edification of the rising generation of Americans, and others who will
follow, it cannot be too often repeated. I can do
no better than to reproduce a portion of an article
written by Florence Howe Hall for the New York
Independent, September 22, 1898. In telling of

"The Building of a Nation's War Hymn," she
says:

"It was in December, 1861, that Mrs. Howe,
in company with her husband, Governor and Mrs.
Andrew, and other friends, visited Washington,
itself almost in the condition of an armed camp.
On their journey thither 'the watch-fires of a hundred circling camps' gleamed in the darkness, the
railroad being paroled by pickets. Mrs. Howe has
told of the martial sights and sounds in the national capital, and of her drive to a distance of
several miles from the city to see a review of our
troops. An attack of the enemy interrupted the
program, and the return drive was made through
files of soldiers, who occupied almost the entire
road. To beguile the tedium of their slow progress,
Mrs. Howe and her friends sang army songs,
among others, 'John Brown's Body.' This seemed
to please the soldiers, who surrounded us like a
river, and who themselves took up the strain, in
the interval crying to us, 'Good for you!' Our
poet had often wished to write words to be sung
to this tune, and now, indeed, had she 'read a fiery
gospel writ in burnished rows of steel.'

"She slept quietly that night; but waking before dawn, found herself weaving together the
lines of a poem, capable of being sung to the 'John

Brown' tune. Line after line, and verse after verse fell into place, and Mrs. Howe, fearing that they would fade from her mind, sprang out of bed, and in the gray half-light hastily wrote down her verses, went back to bed and fell asleep again.

"When she returned to Boston she showed them to James T. Fields, then editor of the Atlantic Monthly. He suggested the title, 'Battle Hymn of the Republic,' and published them promptly. In the Atlantic Monthly for February, 1862, the poem is printed on the first page, but the name of the author is not mentioned; indeed, no names are appended to the table of contents. On the cover of this number the American flag is substituted for the usual design. It may interest practical people to learn that Mrs. Howe received five dollars for her poem."

The writer of the foregoing quotes Rudyard Kipling, himself a man of genius, as describing Mrs. Howe's famous war lyric, as the "terrible Battle Hymn of the Republic." "He saw that only a Republic, a mighty nation of freemen, patient, and slow to wrath, but terrible when once aroused, could have inspired such a song. Yet when in 'The Light That Failed' he makes a group of Englishmen and men of other nationalities sing this hymn as a fitting prelude to their departure for the scene

of war, he recognizes also its universal quality—
a hymn for men of every clime who love liberty
and are willing to lay down their lives for its
sake."

When James Russell Lowell was editor of the
Atlantic Monthly, he declined to publish a poem
written by Mrs. Howe, giving as his reason there-
for that no woman could write a poem, and he said
that "Mrs. Browning's efforts were a conspicuous
illustration of this fact."   But after Mr. Lowell
vacated the editor's chair, Mrs. Howe did write
a poem, and although he wrote many verses which
will live long in our literature, he produced nothing that will last as long, or touch the popular
heart as deeply, as the glorious anthem—

"Mine eyes have seen the glory of the coming of the Lord."

Mrs. Howe says that a printed copy of the
words and music of the song was once sent her
from Constantinople by some person unknown to
her; but afterwards, when she visited Roberts
College, near the Turkish capital, the professors
and their ladies, at parting, asked her to listen
well to what she might hear on her way down the
steep declivity, and to her wonderment she heard,
"in sweet, full cadence, the lines which scarcely
seem mine, so much are they the breath of that

heroic time and of the feeling with which it was filled."

There is a wonderful touch of pathos, as well as patriotism, in this unique battle hymn. Its power over the emotions of men is forcibly exemplified in an incident that took place during the presidential campaign of 1896. United States Senator Thomas C. Platt is known as an intense partisan, and it is not unkind to say of him that he is a master in managing the so-called machine in the Republican politics of New York. At a political gathering, at which the senator was the central figure, if not the controlling spirit, there came a lull in the disputation of the evening, when, in a voice uncultured, of course, but full of feeling that was strangely pathetic, he began the beautiful stanza—

"In the beauty of the lilies Christ was born across the sea."

The other politicians took up the refrain—

"Glory, glory, hallelujah."

The effect was unusually impressive. The asperities of the old political warriors were softened by the hallowed sentiment of the song; and it was said that the result was altogether beyond the power of the charming oratory of Chauncey M. Depew to produce.

I want to quote a few more lines from Florence Howe Hall's excellent paper on the story of the "Battle Hymn of the Republic:" "Unlike many of the songs of the civil war, it contains nothing sectional, nothing personal, nothing of a temporary character. Its author has repeated it to audiences without number, East, West, North and South. While we feel the beauty of the lines and their aspiration after freedom, even in the piping times of peace, it is only in time of storm and stress that their full meaning shines out. Written with intense feeling, they seem to burn and glow when our own emotions are aroused, as they have been of late."

The reader will remember the sudden and extremely sad death of the wife of United States Senator John M. Thurston, of Nebraska, which took place on board the steam yacht Anita, off Sagua la Grande, Cuba, on the 14th of March, 1898. She had gone to Cuba with her husband and a congressional delegation to personally investigate and report upon the situation there. It was a mission of mercy in which Mrs. Thurston took an uncommon interest. She was taken suddenly ill on a stormy sea, and died in a few hours. In her dying moments this broad, noble-hearted woman, made a pathetic appeal for the deliverance

of Cuba from the ruthless hand of Spain. Ten
days later, Mr. Thurston, standing in the Senate
of the United States, said he was there by command of silent lips, to speak once and for all, upon
the Cuban situation; and his masterly plea, for
the freedom of the people that had been beaten
with many stripes, was concluded with the sublime
stanzas so precious to Mrs. Thurston:

"In the beauty of the lilies Christ was born across the sea,
With a glory in his bosom that transfigures you and me;
As he died to make men holy, let us die to make men free,
       While God is marching on."

Mr. Murat Halstead, the widely known journalist, witnessed the execution of John Brown on the
2d of December, 1859, and in an article on "The
Tragedy of John Brown," printed in the New
York Independent, December 1, 1898, he relates
the following interesting incident:

"Something more than ten years later, August,
1870, in Eastern France, I was with the German
invaders of the fair land of Lorraine, and one day
as I looked upon a division of the Grand Army of
the Red Prince, a monstrous mass of men with the
spikes of their helmets and their bayonets glitter-
ing over them under a vast tawny cloud of dust, I
heard with amazement a deep throated burst of
song in English, and it was:

·John Brown's body is mouldering in the ground,
But his soul is marching on,
Glory, hallelujah!'

The German invaders often sang magnificently while marching. German soldiers in our army, in the war of the States, returning to the Fatherland to fight the French, taught their comrades the splendid marching song with which the legions of the North sang along the historic highways of Virginia, that Father Abraham's boys were coming and the soul of John Brown was marching on.''

This soul-inspiring "Battle Hymn of the Republic" was the incarnation of patriotism and martial feeling pent up in the tune of "John Brown's Body." It was struck out of the white heat of unconscious inspiration—the soul's product of a mighty moment. "All through the wild echoes of the fearful struggle" of the civil war, this song was a messenger of faith, hope, and promise. It is indeed the most resonant and elevating of all American battle hymns. It is simple, but dignified, full of vigor, and is worthy of being the imperishable war song of a Christian Nation.

Florence Howe Hall, says: "The soul of the vast army of the American people, struggling for utterance in the greatest crisis of its existence, at last found a voice to express its meaning, and its aspiration—the voice of a woman"—a voice that will ever make the music of patriots

"While God is marching on."

XI.

We are Coming, Father Abraham.

MEASURED by the service it performed at a most critical period during the war between the States, the song entitled, "We are Coming, Father Abraham," deserves a permanent place in the story of the songs of the Union. It was indeed famous in its day and generation, and because it has now largely fallen into disuse, is no reason why its story should not be perpetuated. Any important facts bearing on the life and character of the man who wrote the song, or any stirring event that inspired it, cannot fail to be of special interest.

This country saw some dark days in 1862; and although under previous calls there were fully 500,000 volunteers in the field, a demand for more troops was made by the generals, and on the second of July of that year, President Lincoln

issued a proclamation for 300,000 more. It was
to aid in the filling of the stricken ranks of the
Grand Army of the Republic under that call, that
Mr. John S. Gibbons wrote the rallying song,
which is as follows:

> We are coming, Father Abraham,
>   Three hundred thousand more,
> From Mississippi's winding stream
>   And from New England's shore.
> We leave our plows and workshops,
>   Our wives and children dear,
> With hearts too full for utterance,
>   With but a silent tear.
> We dare not look behind us,
>   But steadfastly before—
> We are coming, Father Abraham,
>   Three hundred thousand more!

> CHORUS.

> We are coming, we are coming,
>   Our Union to restore;
> We are coming, Father Abraham,
>   Three hundred thousand more;
> We are coming, Father Abraham,
>   Three hundred thousand more.

> If you look across the hilltops
>   That meet the northern sky,
> Long, moving lines of rising dust
>   Your vision may descry,
> And now the wind an instant
>   Tears the cloudy veil aside
> And floats our spangled flag
>   In glory and in pride,

And bayonets in the sunlight gleam
    And bands brave music pour—
We are coming, Father Abraham,
    Three hundred thousand more!

If you look all up our valleys
    Where the growing harvests shine,
You may see our sturdy farmer boys
    Fast forming into line;
And children from their mothers' knees
    Are pulling at the weeds,
And learning how to reap and sow,
    Against their country's needs;
And a farewell group stands weeping
    At every cottage door—
We are coming, Father Abraham,
    Three hundred thousand more!

You have called us and we're coming,
    By Richmond's bloody tide,
To lay us down for freedom's sake,
    Our brothers' bones beside;
Or from foul treason's savage grasp
    To wrench the murderous blade,
And in the face of foreign foes,
    Its fragments to parade.
Six hundred thousand loyal men
    And true have gone before—
We are coming, Father Abraham,
    Three hundred thousand more!

Mr. Gibbons was a member of the liberal wing
of the Quaker family called the Hicksites, founded
in the United States by Elias Hicks, about 1827.
He believed in the kind of war the government
was carrying on; and his son-in-law, Mr. James

H. Morse, speaking of Mr. Gibbons' Quakerism in a letter to Mr. Brander Matthews, says he had "a reasonable leaning, however, toward wrath in cases of emergency."

I take the liberty to reproduce from Mr. Matthews' excellent article, in the Century Magazine, on "The Songs of the War," some interesting facts regarding Mr. Gibbons and his ringing call to arms. He lived in New York City, and became an abolitionist, and was one of the editors of the "Anti-Slavery Standard." When the war broke out Mrs. Gibbons and her eldest daughter went to the front and served in the hospitals until the close of the conflict. In the great draft riots in New York City, in 1863, Mr. Gibbons' house was sacked, and to escape the fury of the mob, he and his two youngest daughters made their way over the roofs of houses to Eighth Avenue, where Mr. Joseph H. Choate, now ambassador to Great Britain, had a carriage in waiting for them. It seems that the class of people composing the mob had become exasperated by the great influence of Mr. Gibbons' song in swelling the ranks of the army.

When the call came for 300,000 more volunteers, Mr. Gibbons would take long walks and ponder the matter of writing a song which would meet the extraordinary emergency. He had previously written verse, but was best known as a writer on financial topics, having published two books on banks and banking, and for a while was financial editor of The New York Evening Post. The song did not come by inspiration. It was the product of much thought, and one incident after another was required to give him aid in putting together the lines which were to contribute so much to the uprising of the people in response to the President's call. When the song was finished it was printed in The Evening Post, on the 16th of July, 1862, just two weeks after the proclamation was issued. Mr. Gibbons appears to have had the idea that he would save his reputation by publishing the song anonymously, but it read so well and was in all respects so suited to the times, that at a great mass meeting held in Boston, on the evening after it appeared in New York, the distinguished Josiah Quincy read it as "the latest poem written by William Cullen Bryant." The song was copied far and wide and credited to Mr. Bryant, who was editor of The Post; and it became necessary, in justice to Mr. Gibbons, for Mr. Bryant to publish a note which gave honor to whom honor was due.

The words of the song have been adapted to

music by several composers, but the original
setting by one of the members of the Hutchinson
family, by whom the song was first sung, was the
most stirring of them all. There were some gloomy
days for the government in 1864, when orders for
drafting 700,000 men were issued, and Mr.
Matthews relates an incident that occurred during
the summer of that year which is very pathetic.
One day Lincoln was called down to the Red Room
of the White House to meet some visitors, and
stood with "bowed head, and patient, pensive
eyes," so peculiar to that sad man, while one of
the visitors sang:

> "We are coming, Father Abraham,
> Three hundred thousand more."

Mr. Gibbons died in New York, October 17,
1892.

XII.

A Trio of Good War Songs.

A S the soldier was nerved for the shock of battle by the inspiration in the "Battle Cry of Freedom," so in his prison cell his heart was fired with hope by the cheering strains of—

"Tramp, tramp, tramp, the boys are marching."

And how to the sound of that music the blood still thrills with the enthusiasm of '65. There is forcible suggestion of the solid march of Union armies in the words and music of that familiar song. It was composed by Dr. Root—both words and music—quite early in the war. Its purpose was to give a more hopeful view of the conditions of the country, and more particularly to cheer the boys who had been captured by the enemy and placed in prison pens.

In that remarkable scene at Charleston in the

fall of 1864, we have a striking example of the inspiring power in a song of patriotism. Several hundred of our soldiers were herded in a prison pen. They were half starved, ill-clad, and staggered in their weakness. One afternoon when they were marched out of the pen, but only to exchange one prison for another, there came from these veterans of war, an outburst in the prisoner's song of hope:

"Tramp, tramp, tramp, the boys are marching,
   Cheer up, comrades, they will come,
 And beneath the starry flag we shall breathe the air again,
   Of the freeland in our own beloved home."

These suffering defenders of the Union sang the song not only with patriotic unction, but in splendid triumph, for in a few months after the affecting scenes of that day, they did hear tramp, tramp, tramp, and the boys came marching like conquering heroes, prison doors were unloosed, prison pen walls were broken down, and the boys breathed the air of freedom again.

The Charleston scene teaches us that we can sing away our cares better than we can reason them away; and there are thousands of times in our lives when we put a song under our burdens and they disappear, and we learn to love music for what it makes us forget and for what it makes us

remember.   It has been said that one song in time
of trouble and storm is worth a whole band in ease
and sunshine.   The ministry of song is one of
these beautiful and mighty influences which are
ever illustrated in the highest and divinest life of
man and in the supremest crisis of every nation.

There is more mournful pathos in Dr. Root's
"Just Before the Battle, Mother," than any other
of the thirty or more army songs he composed.
The song whose sentiment was truly pathetic had
a mission in the army as well as the song of humor
—"Wake, Nicodemus"—or the song of cheer—
"Rally Round the Flag."   Dr. Root wrote for
almost all the varied circumstances caused
by the war, and has written for all time as well.
Some one has said, speaking of "Just Before the
Battle, Mother," that "mother and sons are ever
thinking of each other; there is always a war, a
conflict, a battle, a triumph, a blessing somewhere,
and Dr. Root caught its melody and gave it life:"

> Just before the battle, mother,
>   I am thinking most of you,
> While upon the field we're watching
>   With the enemy in view.
> Comrades brave around me lying,
>   Filled with thoughts of home and God,
> For well they know that on the morrow,
>   Some will sleep beneath the sod.

CHORUS.

Farewell, mother, you may never
    Press me to your heart again.
Oh, you'll not forget me, mother,
    If I'm numbered with the slain.

Oh, I long to see you, mother,
    And the loving ones at home,
But I'll never leave our banner
    Till in honor I can come.
Tell the traitors all around you
    That their cruel words we know,
In every battle kill our soldiers
    By the help they give the foe.

Hark! I hear the bugle sounding.
    'Tis the signal for the fight,
Now, may God protect us, mother,
    As he ever does the right.
Hear the "Battle Cry of Freedom,"
    How it swells upon the air!
Oh, yes, we'll rally round the standard
    Or we'll perish nobly there.

I clearly remember how the boys in the Thirty-third Wisconsin Infantry used to sing this song with almost ineffable emotion. In the dullness of camp life and on long and weary marches it appeared to exert a helpful influence that no other song could. The words and music blended so well, and so well interpreted each other in days when many a boy in peril felt all the sentiments the song expressed, that it became one of the great songs of the army.

In "Bright Skies and Dark Shadows," by the Rev. Dr. Henry M. Field, a curious incident is given which took place on the day of the great battle of Franklin, Tenn., November 30, 1864, and was told to Dr. Field on the battle field, by a Mr. McEwen, an old resident at Nashville, at whose house General Kimball made his headquarters, and from the front door of which Mr. McEwen witnessed the whole battle:

"About four o'clock, after the General had left for the field, there lingered a Colonel from Indianapolis in my parlor, who asked my daughters to sing and play a piece of music. I requested the young ladies to sing 'Just Before the Battle, Mother.' As I stepped to the door, a shell exploded within fifty yards. The Colonel immediately sprang to his feet and ran in the direction of his regiment, but before he reached it, or about that time, he was shot, the bullet passing quite through him. He was taken to Nashville, and eighteen days after I received a message from him through an officer, stating the fact of his being shot, and that the piece of music the young women were executing was still ringing in his ears, and had been ever since he left my parlor on the afternoon of the battle. In April, four months later, after the war was over, he had sufficiently recovered to travel, when he came to Franklin, expressly to get the young ladies to finish the song, and relieve his ears. His wife and more than a dozen officers accompanied him. He found the young women and they sang and played the piece through for him in the presence of all the officers, and they wept like children."

Tens of thousands of people in this country and in foreign lands have sung "The Vacant Chair." It is a song of the war that will never grow old. It has carried comfort to many thousands of sorrowing hearts, and its mission will never end. As long as Memorial Day is observed by the American people, and flowers are tenderly laid upon the graves of our fallen heroes, "The Vacant Chair" will be sung. A song we love becomes all the dearer when we know something of the circumstances that gave it birth. Its touching story is well worth repeating and remembering.

The battle of Balls Bluff, Va., in which General McClellan was defeated, was fought on the 21st of October, 1861. In the engagement was the Fifteenth Massachusetts Infantry, commanded by Colonel Charles Devens, who afterwards was Attorney General in President Hayes' Cabinet. The Federal army became demoralized, and a stampede followed. In the Fifteenth Regiment was Lieutenant William F. Grout, only eighteen years old, but brave and manly. There is an account which says that during the battle, while men fell on every side, he escaped unharmed, and that his courage and self-possession urged his men to renewed efforts. When the day was lost and the men were forced to retreat to the river he seemed to be utterly regardless of himself in his desire to have the wounded conveyed to the opposite shore. He crossed the stream with a boat load of sufferers, and, seeing them safely landed, returned to render like assistance to others; but the deadly fire made it necessary to abandon the boats, and he was soon obliged to plunge into the stream to save himself from captivity or death. He had reached the middle of the river when he exclaimed to a comrade near at hand: "Tell Company D I could have reached the shore—but—I'm shot," and the waters immediately closed over him.

Four weeks later Henry S. Washburn, of Worcester, Mass., (now living in Boston at the age of eighty-five) being well acquainted with young Grout, and thinking with deep emotion of the chair that would be vacant at the thanksgiving board in the home of sorrow, wrote the words of the song

in one of these inspired moments, so strange in
their influence—moments in which all the great
songs of the world have been sung, and all the
master discourses pronounced:

We shall meet, but we shall miss him;
    There will be one vacant chair;
We shall linger to caress him
    When we breathe our evening prayer.
When a year ago we gathered
    Joy was in his mild blue eye;
But a golden cord is severed
    And our hopes in ruin lie.

At our fireside, sad and lonely,
    Often will the bosom swell
At remembrance of the story—
    How our noble Willie fell;
How he strove to bear our banner
    Through the thickest of the fight,
And uphold our country's honor
    With the strength of manhood's might.

True, they tell us, wreaths of glory
    Evermore will deck his brow;
But this soothes the anguish only
    Sweeping o'er our heartstrings now.
Sleep to-day, O early fallen!
    In thy green and narrow bed;
Dirges from the pine and cypress
    Mingle with the tears we shed.

We shall meet, but we shall miss him;
    There will be one vacant chair;
We shall linger to caress him
    When we breathe our evening prayer.

In a few weeks after the lines were written Dr. Root set them to music, and the song soon gained international fame. The sad fate of Willie of the song, who fought so well and died so tragically in his youth, is sung in hundreds of thousands of homes here and in foreign lands.

XIII.

Marching through Georgia.

AMONG the songs of the Union which have a
living popularity there is none more deeply
cherished than Work's remarkable song,
"Marching Through Georgia." It came into
being to commemorate one of the most striking
episodes of the war, the famous march of Sherman
from Atlanta to the sea. It was a song of the
last grand effort of the war of the Rebellion, and
from the first it had a powerful influence in
reviving hope and courage during the closing days
of 1864.

In 1841 a man named Alanson Work was
walking along a road in Missouri, when he was
overtaken by some fugitive slaves who asked him
the way to a free state. He directed them, and
responding to their pitiable beseechings, gave them
a little money to aid them in their escape from

Henry C. Work.

bondage. For this he was arrested, tried and convicted, and sentenced to twelve years at hard labor in the state prison at Jefferson City. After serving a term of three or four years he was pardoned on condition that he should return to Connecticut, his native state. But how true are the words of Shakespeare: "Thus the whirligig of time brings his revenges."

One morning in the early months of the war, a young man climbed up to the private room of Dr. George F. Root, in Chicago, with the manuscript of a song for the doctor to examine. He was a tall, care-worn, invalid-like fellow, with sadness in his voice and bearing, and poverty in his dress. The composer looked at the finely written music, and then with astonishment and in pity, he gazed at the forlorn apparition before him, wondering how such a soul as that could produce music. The doctor asked him if he wrote the words and tune, and in a diffident tone, burdened with pathos, he said "yes." He was a printer by trade, but was sickly, and could do but little work. The song was the popular "Kingdom Coming," the first great humorous song of the war. The young man was Henry C. Work, who was nine years old when his father was sentenced to twelve years imprisonment for bestowing charity upon the fugitives. Henry had vivid remembrances of his father's persecution, and had an ardent desire to render some service in the cause of the Union, and Dr. Root encouraged him to write songs for the boys who were strong enough to fight, and his war-pieces became a marvelous power in the army.

The song by Mr. Work, which supersedes all others of his making, was written shortly after General Sherman began his great march from Atlanta to the sea, the movement of the army beginning about the 16th of November, 1864.

Bring the good old bugle, boys,
    We'll sing another song;
Sing it with the spirit
    That will start the world along;
Sing it as we used to sing it,
    Fifty thousand strong,
While we were marching through Georgia.

CHORUS.

Hurrah! hurrah! We bring the jubilee!
Hurrah! hurrah! The flag that makes you free;
So we sang the chorus from Atlanta to the sea
While we were marching through Georgia.

How the darkies shouted
    When they heard the joyful sound,
How the turkeys gobbled
    Which our commissary found,
How the sweet potatoes
    Even started from the ground
While we were marching through Georgia.

Yes, and there were Union men
  Who wept with joyful tears,
When they saw the honored flag
  They had not seen for years,
Hardly could they be restrained
  From breaking forth in cheers,
While we were marching through Georgia.

"Sherman's dashing Yankee boys
  Will never reach the coast,"
So the saucy rebels said.
  It was a handsome boast,
Had they not forgot, alas!
  To reckon with their host,
While we were marching through Georgia.

So we made a thoroughfare
  For freedom and her train,
Sixty miles in latitude,
  Three hundred to the main;
Treason fled before us,
  For resistance was in vain
While we were marching through Georgia.

Mr. Work wrote some splendid army songs,
but his reputation will rest on "Marching
Through Georgia." There are cheering strains
in the music which did much to enliven the camps;
and there is a swinging rhythm about it that kept
in step the marching of the masses. Dr. Root
thought that "Marching Through Georgia" was
more frequently used than any other song of the
war; not so much on account of the intrinsic merit
of its words or music, but because it is retrospec-

tive. "Other war songs, like the 'Battle Cry of
Freedom,' were for exciting a patriotic feeling on
going in the war or in battle, while 'Marching
Through Georgia' is a glorious remembrance on
coming triumphantly out."

In a certain sense, it is the song of all army
songs. It has been said that "age cannot wither
nor custom stale the infinite variety of ways the
tune is served up, from the newsboys on the streets
to the Salvation Army and the tenore-robusto who
sings campaign songs, and from Gilmore's band
to the Dago organ, the gamut of human and arti-
ficial instrumentalities is run with varying
success."

So universal in its use was "Marching Through
Georgia" that General Sherman heard it with
supreme disgust. It pursued him from city to
city, and from state to state; and in all the great
cities of Europe in which he was received with distinguished honors, the burden of the music was
"Marching Through Georgia." When the general
attended the national encampment of the Grand
Army of the Republic in Boston in 1890, he saw
from the reviewing stand two hundred and fifty
bands, and a hundred drum and fife corps pass in
review; and the old warrior stood for seven mortal
hours listening to the never-ending strains of the

music which commemorates the most triumphant
march of modern times. His patience collapsed,
and with a grim gravity, peculiar to him, and in
language too emphatic for repetition here, he declared that he would never attend another national
encampment until every band in the United States
has signed an agreement not to play "Marching
Through Georgia" in his presence. This was
Sherman's last encampment, and when the tune
was next played in his presence, six months after,
"there came no response from the echoless shore
to which his soul had wafted."

The melody of "Marching Through Georgia"
has found its way into nearly every country of the
globe. At a monthly dinner of the Commandery
of the Loyal Legion of the United States, given
in New York City two or three years before General Sherman's death, he related this amusing incident: "Wherever I go, not only in my own country, but in Europe, 'Marching Through Georgia'
pursues me. On one occasion, arriving at a Dublin
hotel in a driving rain, I was congratulating myself that the weather was such as to preclude the
possibility of the usual serenade, and drawing
forth my writing materials, I addressed myself to
my long-neglected correspondence. Scarcely had
I gotten under way, however, when the strains of

that infernal tune smote upon my ear. I sprang
up, and, hustling into my uniform, stepped out
upon the veranda. In the distance a band was
approaching, followed by a number of men with
guns on their shoulders. I advanced to the rail-
ing, and prepared for the pending ovation, but
without a pause, or even a glance toward the spot
where I stood, they went on 'Marching Through
Georgia.' It was a gunning club, so some one told
me afterwards, going to a certain place to shoot at
a target."

There is an expression of enthusiasm in this
war tune which is as fresh now as it was thirty-four
years ago. A story is told that a veteran living in
the backwoods of Ohio was called out to march
with other members of the Grand Army of the
Republic. He had borne the burden and heat of
many days in the civil war, and the hard service
and the weight of years were telling upon him.
After marching a mile or two, the strain became
too severe for the old soldier. His step was uncertain, and he could hardly keep up with the others.
Finally the commander said to him:

"Say, Tom, keep step; you are throwing out
the whole line." "Cap, how kin a feller keep step
to that music?" he replied, pointing to the band
leading the line with one of the popular airs of

the day. "Why don't they play something like
this?" and he hummed, in a voice husky and
scratchy and out of tune, a strain from "Marching Through Georgia." The captain laughed and
turned away, and the introductory notes of the next
piece caused the old fellow to straighten up. His
cudgel waved about like the baton of a drum-major,
and a little later a thousand feet were coming down
as one; the fatigue of the march was forgotten, and
a thousand voices were joined in the rousing
chorus.

Henry Clay Work was born at Middletown,
Conn., in 1832. He had received a common school
education, and in 1855 settled in Chicago, where
he continued his trade as a printer. He began to
write songs quite early in his young manhood, and
one of his first compositions was "Lily Dale,"
which, it is said, brought him $2,500. During his
life he wrote seventy-five songs, but not being at
his best at all times, many of them have passed
away with the impulse or the occasion that produced them, and are now forgotten.

Mr. Work's fame as a writer of songs began
with the breaking out of the civil war. As already
stated, his first humorous song of the war was
"Kingdom Coming," then followed "Wake Nicodemus," "Babylon is Fallen," "Drafted Into the

Army," "Brave Boys Are They," "Song of a Thousand Years," and the last, but greatest of all, "Marching Through Georgia." As there was a tender ministry in such a song as "Just Before the Battle, Mother," so there was a special ministry of good cheer in the humorous pieces composed by Mr. Work which saved thousands of soldiers from despair. Apropos of our jocular war songs, the Russian battle hymn is usually a mournful thing, and an American traveler says that when a man has been compelled to hear a Russian war melody, it will make him mad enough to fight somebody if he had to walk a thousand miles to find his man.

The popularity and frequent use of "Marching Through Georgia" have overshadowed all other songs of the war written or composed by Mr. Work. Among his best compositions was "Song of a Thousand Years," written when the war-cloud was lowest and darkest and when the cause of the Union did not have the friendly sympathy of England. Of course, the words are now obsolete. There are no "desponding freemen;" no "needless fears to fling to the winds;" no "envious foes beyond the ocean;" no "rebels to hide their faces;" and no "secret traitors to creep back to their dens."

The visit of President McKinley to the South in the autumn of 1898, "meant full reconciliation

of the surviving veterans of the Blue and the Gray,
their sons and grandsons, over the shriven ashes
of their dead comrades on both sides. His kindly
words broke the seal of the sepulchre in which
Southern loyalty had been buried with the ashes
of its dead heroes, and gave a new resurrection to
its ancient love for the flag of their fathers. They
smote the rock of Southern prejudice and from it
gushed forth the living waters of patriotic sentiment so long locked up." Therefore the words of
"Song of a Thousand Years" are out of harmony
with our new relations. But the music is stately
and vigorous, and should be set to nobler words.
If some poet of the soul could be inspired to produce lines which would give expression to the highest patriotism, or to praise that is the symbol of
perpetual gladness, and wed them to the melody
of "Song of a Thousand Years," it would give
meritorious honor to one of our best tunes of the
civil war.

The last years of Henry C. Work were full of
sadness. Accumulating a handsome competence
from the sale of his war songs, he went to Europe
in 1865, and spent two years in travel. It was
during his stay abroad that he was married,
although there is a conflict of opinion as to the
time, there being no written account of the event.

In 1867 he settled in Vineland, N. J., and in connection with an elder brother, invested a large part of his fortune in a fruit farm. While living in Vineland his first child died, and a second was born to him. Work was never a hopeful man, and when his little boy was taken away the melancholy which had been too often his companion, came upon him in a worse form than ever before. It was about this time that his wife's mind became seriously affected, which made it necessary to take her to an asylum for the insane. Work was overwhelmed by this calamity, and when his little property in Chicago was swept away by the fire of 1871, and his investment in Vineland went down in the vortex that had sunk many other fortunes, the sad man became a wanderer upon the earth. When he saw that all was gone, the only comment he made on his adversities was: "It is well; had I become rich I might have become hard." But in his sorrow and despondency Mr. Work judged himself too harshly. He was a sympathetic man by nature, was always kind and gentle, and was generous to a fault in his giving.

Mr. Cady, formerly of Root & Cady, music publishers of Chicago, relates the story that he went to New York shortly after the Chicago fire to go into business for himself, and concluded that if he could get a new song from Work it would be helpful to both. He began a search for the composer, and at last found him reading proof in a printing house. When Mr. Cady said to him, "Henry, I want you to write me a song," the latter, hardly able to control his emotions, answered, "I have no heart to write songs again." But Mr. Cady encouraged him to consent, and in a few days Mr. Work handed him "My Grandfather's Clock," "Sweet Echo Dell," and one of a spiritual nature, "Life Beyond the Veil." In handing them to Mr. Cady he remarked that he considered them of little merit, holding the latter piece, however, as the best. The last two did not reach a heavy sale, and Mr. Work was deeply disappointed because "Life Beyond the Veil" was not appreciated. "My Grandfather's Clock" was a success from the start, and nearly a quarter of a million copies were sold.

After the appearance of "My Grandfather's Clock" in the latter part of 1875, Mr. Work seemed to lead an aimless life. This was his last song worthy of mention. He lived in self-imposed retirement in New York City, and at times went to Hartford, Conn., to visit his aged mother, and it was on one of these occasions that he was taken unexpectedly ill, and passed away on the 8th of June, 1884.

It has been written that there is a way to make life so true that when "the sunset is nearing, with its murky vapor and lowering skies, the very clouds of sorrow may be fringed with golden light." But Mr. Work could not find that way, neither could he understand the philosophy which teaches that adversity is sent for our instruction. The rarest birds are those that sing sweetest in time of storm; and the songs which have the most powerful hold on human affection and will longest endure, have come from the hearts of men and women when their sorrows were keenest and life's way darkest. But, unfortunately, Work could not command himself in the storm of disappointment, and was beaten back; and the voice that once sang for the inspiration of the Union in the winter of war, was silenced in the winter of his own life.

Old Shady.

XIV

Old Shady—The Famous Singing Cook.

PERHAPS the most fun-provoking song of the civil war is "Old Shady." With a fine bass or baritone voice behind it, it is over-running with laughter. To announce the piece at a war song concert, or at a public entertainment of any kind, is to create a flutter of pleasant anticipation and to signify to the auditors that merriment may have full swing.

During the siege of Vicksburg, in May and June of 1863, a great many slaves had escaped within the Union lines. Some of them were hired by the officers in various departments of the army, and many others were given free transportation North. Among those serving as cooks was a slave, almost white, who was known by the name of "Old Shady." He was employed at the headquarters of General McPherson during the siege, and was a fine specimen of simple, honest manhood. General Sherman, in an article in The North American Review, says "Old Shady" was a poet in the rough. After supper, the officers at headquarters, including several generals, and Mrs. Grant and Mrs. Sherman, would assemble to hear him and his chorus of darkies sing. One of the songs became very popular, and was personal to the negro cook, entitled, "Day of Jubilee," but now better known as "Old Shady," which ran thus:

> Oh, yah, yah, darkies, laugh wid me,
> Fur de white folks say Ole Shady's free,
> So don't you see dat de jubilee
> Is a-coming, coming—Hail mighty day!

> CHORUS.

> Den away, den away, I can't stay here no longer,
> Den away, den away, for I am going home.

> Oh, mass' got scared and so did his lady,
> Dis chile breaks fur Ole Uncle Aby;
> "Open de gates, out here's Ole Shady
> A-coming, coming"—Hail mighty day!

> Goodby, Mass' Jeff, goodby Mis'r Stephens,
> 'Scuse dis niggah fur takin' his leavins,
> 'Spect purty soon you'll hear Uncle Abram's
> Coming, coming—Hail mighty day!

> Goodby, hard work, wid never any pay,
> I'ze a-gwine up north where de good folks say
> Dat white wheat bread and a dollar a day
> Are coming, coming—Hail mighty day!

Oh, I've got a wife and I've got a baby,
Livin' up yonder in Lower Canady,
Won't dey laugh when dey see Ole Shady
A-coming, coming—Hail mighty day!

General Sherman, speaking of "Old Shady,"
says: "I do not believe that since the Prophet
Jeremiah bade the Jews to sing with gladness for
Jacob, and to shout among the chiefs of the nations, because of their deliverance from the house
of bondage, any truer song of gladness ever as-
cended from the lips of man than at Vicksburg,
where 'Old Shady' sang for us in a voice of pure
melody this song of deliverance from the bonds of
slavery."

The general was a great admirer of the negro
character, because, as a rule, the colored people
were kind and respectful; and he quotes Henry
Clay as saying that his colored boy, whose name
is now forgotten, was "the most accomplished gentleman in America." General Sherman then
adds: "What more beautiful sentiment than that
of my acquaintance, 'Old Shady:' 'Good-bye,
Massa' Jeff;' 'good-bye, Massa' Stephens;' "scuse
dis niggar for takin' his leavin's'—polite and
gentle to the end. Burns never said anything
better."

The name of "Old Shady" was D. Blakeley

Durant, and after the war he got his "wife and nice little baby out of the lower Canady" and worked on an upper Mississippi steamboat. General Sherman once met him on one of the river steamers, when "he sang from the hurricane deck that good old song, which brought tears to the eyes of the passengers. I believe him now dead, but living or dead, he has the love and respect of the old army of the Tennessee which gave him freedom. 'Good-bye, Massa' Jeff; good-bye, Massa' Stephens;' was a beautiful expression of the faithful family servant who yearned for freedom and a 'dollar a day.'" General Sherman's article for The Review was written in 1888, and Durant did not die until 1896. After working on the river boats for some time, he settled at North Forks, North Dakota, where he established a comfortable home, and where one of his daughters was graduated from the North Dakota state university.

The tune to which the words of "Old Shady" are now sung was composed by B. R. Hanby, an interesting character and a man of great musical talent. He wrote "Darling Nellie Gray," by which he is best known. He was just beginning to make a name for himself in the musical world, when he was stricken down in the prime of young manhood.

XV

Tenting on the Old Camp Ground.

ONE Sunday evening in 1896, Mr. Grasheider sang "Tenting on the Old Camp Ground" at Trinity church, Chicago, and the effect on the audience was so remarkable that it called out an editorial in The Tribune on the influence of that popular song of the civil war. On the occasion referred to, the song moved the fountain of tears in the soldiers and others who were present, recalling, as it did, many a scene in the Southland in the old battle days, so long ago, and yet so near. The melody is of that peculiar quality which will prevent the song from ever growing too old to reach the emotions of the human heart.

In December, 1894, I lectured in Music Hall, Kansas City, Mo., on "The Story of Patriotic Songs." A special feature of the program was the singing of some of the great battle hymns and na-

tional songs whose history and illustrations of their
influence were given in the lecture. The audience was quite large, and among those who honored
me with their presence were members from three
ex-Confederate posts. After giving the story of
"Tenting on the Old Camp Ground," Captain
Henry, a popular singer, and editor of a soldier's
paper, began the song in a tone full of genuine feeling. The audience was requested to join in the
refrain:

> "Many are the hearts that are weary to-night,
> Wishing for the war to cease."

It was extremely affecting to hear that large
gathering of old soldiers of both armies give expression to their sentiment by singing this song
of affection with a perfect unison of hearts as well
as of voices. I cannot recall another instance when
the chorus of "Tenting on the Old Camp Ground"
was sung with more soul-feeling, with finer
rhythm, or with more exquisite harmony, than by
that audience composed of the Blue and the Gray.

Two or three years ago The Chicago Inter-
Ocean printed several communications on the
authorship of this song. One writer claimed that
it was written on the night of the battle of Cedar
Creek Hill, Va., and that Kittredge wrote the
words, while his comrade, named Russell, com-

posed the music. In order to get a story of the song stripped of all fiction, I wrote to Mr. Kittredge requesting the essential facts connected with its birth, and on the 2d of May, 1897, he wrote from his home at Reed's Ferry, N. II., as follows :

"I take this time to give you a little history of 'Tenting on the Old Camp Ground.' I wrote the words and music at the same time one evening, soon expecting to go down South to join the boys in blue, and I desired to have something to sing for them, as that had been my profession, giving concerts for a few years before the war. I think I wrote the song in tears, thinking of my wife and little daughter; but I was not accepted when examined by the physician. He thought I could do my part better to sing for Uncle Sam, so I kept writing and singing for Liberty and Union. The song was composed in 1863, and published by Ditson, Boston, in 1864.

"WALTER KITTREDGE."

Mr. Kittredge was born in Merrimac, N. H., in 1832. At the age of twenty he began to give ballad concerts, and four years later he sang with Joshua Hutchinson, of the noted Hutchinson family. After the war broke out in 1861, he compiled a "Union Song Book," which was only a moderate success. His only composition which had merit enough to keep it alive is "Tenting on the Old Camp Ground." Like many other singers, Kittredge is a "poet" of one song only, and his fame rests solely upon the product of a sudden "inspiration"—if that term is permissible in this connection.

"Tenting on the Old Camp Ground" is not an animating battle piece, of course, but is peculiarly touching in sentiment and plaintive in melody; and many thousands of soldiers, in the monotony of camp life and on weary marches, when thoughts of home burdened the mind, found relief in its pathetic tones and in the delightful harmony of the chorus. Such a song has a powerful hold upon human feelings. It touches the better part of our natures, and "Tenting on the Old Camp Ground," though not a song that has made exciting history, will be long and affectionately associated with the patriotic struggle for liberty and Union.

XVI.

Songs of Cheer and Pathos.

AMONG the fine songs of cheer which the war times produced, "When Johnny Comes Marching Home" was one of the most popular. It was a great favorite in the homes of the North, and nowhere did it cause more genuine merriment than in the army when the boys were either on the march or in camp. The four stanzas are as follows:

> When Johnnie comes marching home again,
> > Hurrah! Hurrah!
> We'll give him a hearty welcome then,
> > Hurrah! Hurrah!
> > The men will cheer, the boys will shout,
> > The ladies they will all turn out,
> > And we'll all feel gay
> > When Johnnie comes marching home.
>
> The old church bell will peal with joy,
> > Hurrah! Hurrah!
> To welcome home our darling boy,
> > Hurrah! Hurrah!

The village lads and lassies gay,
With roses they will strew the way,
And we'll all feel gay
When Johnnie comes marching home.

Get ready for the jubilee,
            Hurrah!   Hurrah!
We'll give the hero three times three,
            Hurrah!   Hurrah!
The laurel wreath is ready now
To place upon his loyal brow,
And we'll all feel gay
When Johnnie comes marching home.

Let love and friendship on that day,
            Hurrah!   Hurrah!
Their choicest treasures then display,
            Hurrah!   Hurrah!
And let each other perform some part,
To fill with joy the warrior's heart,
And we'll all feel gay
When Johnnie comes marching home.

In all the war song books in which "When
Johnny Comes Marching Home" is found, the
authorship has been credited to "Louis Lambert."
The reader will be surprised, perhaps, to know
that this was the *nom de plume* of Patrick S. Gilmore, the great bandmaster and projector of the
Boston Peace Jubilee of 1869 and 1872.   The
song was written in 1863, and its rousing refrain
still gives it a hold on the ears of the people.
There is such a rattling good quality in the music,

Charles Carroll Sawyer.

that it has found its way in several European countries where its use is very frequent.

Mr. Gilmore, who died in 1892, wrote another song during the war, "Good News from Home," which gained a popularity that was almost world-wide for several years.

There were two songs widely sung in the South as well as in the North during the war, "When this Cruel War is Over," and "Who Will Care for Mother Now?" They were written by Charles C. Sawyer of Brooklyn, New York, who began writing sonnets when he was twelve years old. During the war he composed many songs, which, on account of the absence of sectional or party sentiment, became great favorites among the soldiers of both armies.

The first of Mr. Sawyer's songs is entitled, "Weeping, Sad and Lonely," but is more generally known as "When this Cruel War is Over:"

> Dearest love, do you remember
>   When we last did meet,
> How you told me that you loved me,
>   Kneeling at my feet?
> Oh, how proud you stood before me,
>   In your suit of blue,
> When you vowed to me and country
>   Ever to be true.

Weeping, sad and lonely,
  Hopes and fears, how vain!
Yet praying, when this cruel war is over,
  Praying that we meet again!

When the summer breeze is sighing
  Mournfully along,
Or when autumn leaves are falling,
  Sadly breathes the song.
Oft in dreams I see thee lying
  On the battle plain,
Lonely, wounded, even dying,
  Calling, but in vain.

The second song, "Who Will Care for Mother
Now?" is as follows:

Why am I so weak and weary?
  See how faint my heated breath.
All round to me seems darkness.
  Tell me, comrades, is this death?
Ah, how well I know your answer!
  To my fate I meekly bow,
If you'll only tell me truly
  Who will care for mother now?

Soon with angels I'll be marching,
  With bright laurels on my brow;
I have for my country fallen.
  Who will care for mother now?

Who will comfort her in sorrow?
  Who will dry the falling tear,
Gently smooth her wrinkled forehead?
  Who will whisper words of cheer?

Even now I think I see her
  Kneeling, praying for me!   How
Can I leave her in her anguish?
  Who will comfort mother now?

Let this knapsack be my pillow,
  And my mantle be the sky;
Hasten, comrades, to the battle,
  I will like a soldier die.
Soon with angels I'll be marching,
  With bright laurels on my brow,
I have for my country fallen,
  Who will care for mother now?

This song is said to have been suggested by the recollection of a bloody battle. Whether this is true or not, makes little difference. It became immensely popular, and it is claimed that these two songs and "Mother Would Comfort Me," also written by Mr. Sawyer, had an aggregate sale of three million copies during the war.

The Federal Union, a journal published at Milledgeville, Ga., makes the following comments on Mr. Sawyer's songs of the war: "Charles Carroll Sawyer is one of the most gifted sons of the North. His songs gush from his soul as naturally as the water gushes from the mountain rock, and they are just as pure, sweet, and refreshing. His sentiments are fraught with the greatest tenderness and never one word has he written about the South or the war that could wound the sore chords of the Southern heart. We trust that his songs will be sung and his exquisite airs will be warbled and played throughout our sunny regions, and that the heart of the South will rise up to shake hands with all such hearts as his whenever and wherever they meet them, or from whatsoever point of the compass they hail."

Mr. Sawyer was a very useful war poet, although he did not write anything distinctively great like Julia Ward Howe, George F. Root, Henry C. Work, or Walter Kittredge. But his songs served a noble purpose, and their kindly influence will be long remembered. He died at his home in Brooklyn, October 3d, 1891, at the age of fifty-eight years.

The incidents given in the preceding pages show how important is the history made by these national songs and battle hymns. The story of their influence should never grow dull to the American people. Like the deeds of devotion and heroism which saved the Union, these songs should live forever to make the American character devoted and heroic. They teach the highest form of patriotism, from which young men and women of to-day can learn much which will inspire higher manhood and womanhood.

I think that we are yet too near the civil war

to comprehend the fulness of its greatness, or the true value of its songs. When that strife, and the patriotic spirit it evoked, are a long distance in the past, the historians will write of these grand songs of the Union in a way which will make them the most interesting of all the great transactions of history.

In part adopting the sentiment of another, "this America of ours is the Mt. Sinai of the nations;" and if the divine law of liberty, and one flag, and an inseverable national bond of patriotism and unity have proceeded out of the terrible thunder and lightning of its great struggle, it is in a large sense because the grand passions of the soul in that conflict, found expression in songs of mighty power, which inspired loyalty and courage, and made the way to victory easier.

XVII

Home, Sweet Home.

BIANCOLELLI, the celebrated buffoon, kept
Paris audiences in a roar of laughter, while
he himself was dying with melancholy.
Work wrote the most gladsome song of the rebellion period, "Marching Through Georgia," but
was the saddest of all our war poets. Blacklock,
in his majestic hymn, "Come, O My Soul! in
Sacred Lays," had a beautiful conception of God
in the stars and "enthroned amid the radiant
spheres," but he never saw the glory of the stars,
the beauty of a summer sky, or the splendor of the
noonday sun. Payne wrote the loveliest home song
the world ever sang, "Home, Sweet Home," but
not after the age of thirteen, when his mother died,
did he know what it was to have a home, and closed

John Howard Payne.

his strange life on the distant shores of the Mediterranean.

John Howard Payne was born in the city of New York in 1792. At a very early age he developed a taste for literature and the stage. At seventeen he appeared at the old Park theater in New York, and filled many engagements in other cities as the "American Juvenile Wonder." He went to England when twenty-one, and afterwards to France, and remained abroad for twenty years. In Paris he took up his abode in a garret on the topmost story of a house, and although he seems to have met with fair success in London, he was poor, and many times wretched. During his years in London and Paris he appears to have been diligent in the business of writing dramas, particularly translating from the French. A batch of these adaptations was sold to Charles Kemble of Covent Garden theater, London, in 1823, for £230, of that amount £30 being paid for "Clari; or the Maid of Milan." It was in this opera that one song was found that melted the heart of London and of the world, and the plaintive melody is everywhere familiar, and everywhere its tender pathos invests with affectionate regard the memory of John Howard Payne:

'Mid pleasures and palaces though we may roam,
Be it ever so humble, there's no place like home!
A charm from the skies seems to hallow us there,
Which, seek through the world, is ne'er met with elsewhere,
            Home! home! sweet, sweet home!
There's no place like home; there's no place like home.

An exile from home splendor dazzles in vain,
Oh! give me my lowly, thatch'd cottage again;
The birds singing gaily, that come at my call;
Give me them, with the peace of mind, dearer than all.
            Home! home! sweet, sweet home!
There's no place like home; there's no place like home.

How sweet 'tis to sit 'neath a fond father's smile,
And the cares of a mother to soothe and beguile.
Let others delight 'mid new pleasures to roam,
But give me, Oh! give me the pleasures of home.
            Home! home! sweet, sweet home!
But give me, Oh! give me the pleasures of home.

To thee I'll return, over-burdened with care,
The heart's dearest solace will smile on me there;
No more from that cottage again will I roam,
Be it ever so humble, there's no place like home.
            Home! home! sweet, sweet home!
There's no place like home; there's no place like home.

The opera was enormously prosperous and made fortunes for all concerned in it except the always unfortunate and dependent writer of the song.

There has been much controversy over the authorship of the beautiful melody of "Home, Sweet Home," and to enter into a discussion as to who was the composer, would be needless, as it would be uninteresting. It is sufficient to quote a brief article from Charles Mackay, the distinguished English poet and journalist. In writing to The London Telegraph, he says: "With the view of putting an end to these controversies about the authorship of the melody of 'Home, Sweet Home' once for all, I write this letter to prove to the most incredulous that the air is English, and was the composition of the very eminent and gifted musician, the late Sir Henry R. Bishop. In one of the many conversations on well-known English melodies with that gentleman, I took occasion to ask him for information on the subject of 'Home, Sweet Home,' the authorship of which was often attributed to him, and as often denied by many, who claimed it as a national Sicilian air which Sir Henry had discovered and rearranged. He therefore favored me with the whole history. He had been engaged in his early boyhood to edit a collection of the national melodies of all countries. In the course of his labors he discovered that he had no Sicilian melody worthy of reproduction, and Sir Henry thought he would invent one. The result was the now well-known air of 'Home, Sweet Home,' which he composed to the verses of an American author, Mr. Howard Payne, then residing in England. When the collection was published the melody became so popular that, to use a common phrase, 'it took the town by storm,' and several musical publishers, believing it to be Sicilian, and non-copyrighted, reissued it."

The universality of the words made the song greatly successful; and one authority has it that one hundred thousand copies were sold in a single year, and that within two years after its publication the song had yielded the original publishers a net profit of $10,000. It secured for Miss M. Tree, who was the first person to sing "Home, Sweet Home," a husband, and a mansion filled with plenty; while the writer of the song was in a lonely and almost hopeless struggle with pinching want. It is claimed that he not only lost the £25 which was to have been paid him for the copyright on the twentieth performance of the "Maid of Milan," but was not even complimented with a copy of his own song by the publishers.

Payne continued his residence in London until 1832, when his ill-success led him to return to the United States. In New York, and several other cities, he was honored with several substantial benefits. Although he was a fair actor in certain characters, and a dramatist of no mean ability, he seems to have been inclined to the heresy that the world owed him a living. With all his varied talents, which were ample enough to give him success in his profession if rightly applied, the eight or nine years following his return to this country show an unsatisfactory record.

In 1841 he visited Washington and made application for a position in the consular service. He was a burden to his friends, and the administration hesitated to entrust a consulate in his hands. One day while Mr. Webster, secretary of state, was temporarily absent, his son, Fletcher— then his private secretary and afterwards commander of the famous Twelfth Massachusetts, the "John Brown" regiment of the civil war— appointed Payne consul to Tunis, in Northern Africa. This caused no end of trouble. Full of the dignity of his office, he wanted the government to convey him to the scene of his future labors in a vessel of war. President Tyler denied the request, and Payne was in a state of despair, and it was only by the aid of his friends that he was able to cross the Atlantic. He was next heard of in Paris, destitute, and living on a friend. An American who had met Payne in Washington, but was only slightly acquainted with him, loaned him money enough to carry him to Tunis. His administration of the office of consul was more in the nature of a farce than serious diplomatic business, and shortly after President Polk was inaugurated in 1845, Payne was relieved and returned to the United States. During the following six years he subsisted mainly on the hospitality of his friends, and partly on his deficient income from his contributions to the press.

It was during the closing part of his last visit to this country, in December, 1850, that Payne witnessed the most brilliant and soul-stirring scene in all the course of his checkered life. Jenny Lind, under the management of P. T. Barnum, was making her triumphant tour through the United States. She gave her two concerts in Washington, and one of them was heard in the hall of the house of representatives. The audience at the capitol represented the finest ability in the land. President Fillmore and family, the members of the cabinet, judges of the supreme court, senators and representatives, and foreign ambassadors, were among those who had assembled to hear the sweetest song angel the world had ever produced. The Philadelphia Record of that time gave an interesting account of the event: "No common poet ever received a more enviable compliment than was paid to John Howard Payne by Jenny Lind on her last visit to his native land. It was in the great national hall of the city of Washington where the most distinguished audience that had ever been seen in the capital of the republic was assembled. The matchless singer entranced the vast throng with her most exquisite melodies—'Casta Diva,' the 'Flute Song,' the 'Bird Song,' and 'Greeting to America.' But the great feature of the occasion seemed to be an act of inspiration. The singer suddenly turned her face to the part of the auditorium where Payne was sitting and sang 'Home, Sweet Home' with such pathos and power that a whirlwind of excitement and enthusiasm swept through the vast audience. Daniel Webster himself almost lost his self-control, and one might readily imagine that Payne thrilled with rapture at this unexpected and magnificent rendition of his own immortal lyric."

The spirit of Payne was ever restless, and a Whig administration having come into power since his removal from office in 1845, he asked for a diplomatic post more in harmony with his desires than that in Africa, but in this he failed, and was returned to Tunis in 1851 by President Fillmore. But his tenure of office was brief, his death having occurred on the 10th of April, 1852. He was buried in the cemetery of St. George at Tunis, and a suitable monument was erected to his memory, which bore this inscription:

"In memory of Colonel John Howard Payne, twice consul of the United States of America for the city and kingdom of Tunis, this stone is here placed by a grateful country. He died in the American Consulate in this city after a tedious illness, April 10, 1852."

But Payne's "restlessness did not end with his life." His ashes no longer lie on the shores of the Mediterranean. In 1883, through the beneficence of William W. Corcoran, the noted philanthropist of Washington, the remains of Payne were borne across the sea in a French steamer to find a resting place in the capital city of his native land. The burial took place in Oak Hill cemetery, on a beautiful Sunday, the 10th of June, 1883, and the benediction of the ceremony was the blending of one thousand voices and instruments in the immortal melody of "Home, Sweet Home."

The city of Washington had seen many funeral pageants, but none more striking than that of the re-interment of the man who had died long ago, far from his native land, unnoticed and unknown. Presidents and senators and statesmen of every degree had been borne through the streets with every sign of respectful sorrow, but never was a dead poet, famous only for a single song, so honored. "There are hundreds of monuments of distin-

guished men in Washington who were very conspicuous, and some of whom performed great and
memorable services. But no monument there will
be visited by a greater throng of pilgrims, and no
memory will appeal more tenderly to all of them,
than that of the wandering actor who lived and
died alone, and of whom nothing is remembered
but that he wrote one song."

An odd story of "Home, Sweet Home" has
been going the rounds of the papers during the
past few years, and has been copied approvingly
by such estimable publications as the Youth's Companion and the New York Christian Advocate.
Briefly told, the story is as follows:

"The first time that the tender lyric, 'Home,
Sweet Home,' was sung in public was when an Indian, brooding over the death of his beloved squaw
and papoose, committed suicide on the spot where
they were buried.

"It was a time when the boundary lines between Georgia and Tennessee were in dispute, and
the half-breeds were constantly making trouble.
In order to harmonize contending factions, our
government established a trading post there. John
Howard Payne appeared on the scene, and on sus-
picion of inciting the Indians to insubordination,
was arrested and carried to the council house.

"With others he witnessed the burial of the heart-broken Indian, and began softly singing to himself the song which has since echoed through every land on earth." The sequel is told by The Atlanta Constitution in these words:

"General Bishop, who had kept a close scrutiny on his actions, heard the song and called Payne to him.

" 'Young man,' said the stern old Indian fighter, 'where did you learn that song ?'

" 'I wrote that song myself,' replied Payne.

" 'And where did you get the tune ?'

" 'I composed that also.'

" 'Would you let me have a copy of it ?'

" 'Certainly I will.'

" 'Well, a man who can sing and write like that is no incendiary. Appearances may be against you, but I am going to set you free. I shall write out your discharge immediately, and a pass to carry you anywhere you choose through the nation.'

"Payne had been housed at the home of a family living near by, and on his return there he exhibited his pass and related the circumstances. That was the first time that 'Home, Sweet Home' had ever been sung in public."

The sentiment of the story may be charming,

but the whole transaction, as related by The Constitution, is a piece of wretched fiction. The narrative does not rise to the level of even tradition or legend. That such an incident could not have taken place is seen from the fact that Payne went to Europe in 1813, when he was twenty-one years old, and remained there until 1832. He wrote "Home, Sweet Home" in Paris when making a translation of the "Maid of Milan," and the song was first sung at Covent Garden theater, London, on the 8th of May, 1823. When Payne first visited the United States after writing the song, he was forty years old, and therefore could not be the young man of the Indian story. More than that, Payne never was so idiotic as to claim that he composed the melody of the song.

The following incident illustrating the triumph of "Home, Sweet Home" is a fitting close to the story of the song:

In Northern Georgia during the civil war the two great armies confronted each other, and had rested on their arms for the night. Their skirmishing lines had met during the day, and a battle was imminent on the morrow. At eight o'clock one of the Federal bands struck up "The Star Spangled Banner," which evoked prolonged cheers from the Union side. When its echoes were

lost in the distance the Confederate bands started
the sprightly air of "Dixie," which was welcomed
with a vigorous Southern yell. The Federals replied with "Hail Columbia," and in quick response
came "Maryland, My Maryland." "Yankee
Doodle" then broke out upon the evening air; the
other side sent back the "Bonnie Blue Flag," and
the surrounding hills echoed with the "Battle
Hymn of the Republic." The moments of impressive silence which followed this friendly contest of war tunes were broken only by the Confederate bands, when "calm on the listening ear of
night," came the soft, sweet strains of "Home,
Sweet Home." Its exquisite sentiment, its
pathetic tenderness, vividly recalled to the minds
of the soldiers the dearest spot on earth, where they
had left their hearts; and the Union bands joined
in the music of the universal song. For the moment sectional lines were obliterated, and passion
was softened by the controlling and melting tones
of the world's great refrain:

> "Home! home! sweet, sweet home!
> There's no place like home; there's no place like home."

Then followed an outburst of applause from the
Blue and the Gray, and for once their hearts beat
in unison, and the voices of the two armies rose in
sweet concord in that deathless song which goes to

the human heart wherever love and home are
known. There was no other power outside of the
realm of the miraculous but "Home, Sweet Home,"
that could have united the hearts and voices of
those two hostile armies.

XVIII.

Songs of the South—Dixie.

TWO or three years ago the Southern papers
were discussing the interesting fact that com-
paratively few of the songs of the South are
the products of Southern writers. A woman long
a resident of Tennessee, and who has given the
subject much careful study, says the characteristic
Southern songs, such as "Suwannee River," "Old
Folks at Home," "Nellie Gray," "Massa's in the
Cold, Cold Ground," and other familiar songs
cherished by Southern people, were written in the
North. She adds that even the "Mocking Bird,"
and the beautiful music of "Maryland, My Maryland," were written by a Philadelphian, and that
the composer of "Dixie" is a man who, so far as
known, never lived in Dixie.

It is extraordinary that the South, with its
well known literary taste, should be deficient in

Daniel D. Emmett.

songs. The explanation given by The Nashville
Banner is the lack of musical education among the
men of the South. Musical advantages are offered
to the Southern girls, but Southern young men are
seldom encouraged to take a musical education.
The Banner evidently believes that the successful
song writers are limited to the male persuasion.
While there are some notable exceptions, history
shows this to be substantially true. It is, nevertheless, a little remarkable, as one writer says, that a
great section of the country, having such distinc-
tive traits and characteristics, should be so little
represented by native song writers.

It is conceded on all hands that "Dixie" is the
most popular of the songs of the South. It was
not a product of the war, and was not made in the
South; but a peculiar and fortuitous circumstance
led to its adoption by the Confederate army in
1861, and it soon carried the people into a state
of impassioned emotion, and to-day its popularity
is so great that in reality it has become one of the
songs of the Union. President Lincoln had great
admiration for the tune, possibly because he heard
it sung to Republican words in the never-to-be-
forgotten campaign of 1860. Shortly after the
surrender at Appomattox, he requested the band
to play "Dixie," pleasantly remarking that "as we

have captured the Confederate army, we have also captured the Confederate tune, and both belong to us."

There has been considerable dispute over the authorship of "Dixie," and to make its interesting story as clear and concise as possible, and at the same time true to history, I quote from an article written in 1895 by Mr. Edward W. Bok, the distinguished editor of The Ladies' Home Journal, and first published, I believe, in The Pittsburg Dispatch:

"It is a fact not widely known that Daniel D. Emmett, the venerable and retired minstrel, author of 'Dixie,' is now living in Mount Vernon, Ohio. If he survives another anniversary of his birth he will round out eighty years, having been born in the place where he lives on October 29, 1815.

"Emmett is full of little anecdotes of the two great Shermans, William T. and John, who used to go to school at Gambier, near Mount Vernon, and has many fond recollections of romps about the hills with them, of the great times they had at playing 'shinney,' and how the Sherman boys were never allowed both to be on the same side, for they were both leaders and were better separated and leading opposite forces.

"Mr. Emmett says that it was a fashion in

those days among the young people to try their skill at making verses and to sing them to some popular tune. 'Jim Crow' was a favorite in those days, and the boys and girls found great delight in fitting and rhyming words to sing to that tune. In this way, Mr. Emmett formed a taste for verse-making and singing, which later led him to minstrelsy. Mr. Emmett made his own verses and sang them to some popular tune. He traveled all over the United States, and was the favorite minstrel everywhere he went. His understanding of the negro dialect was perfect, as was likewise his rendering. His love of minstrelsy is still visible in him. His voice is thoroughly trained to the sweet tone of the melodious darky's voice, and a few old darky expressions and songs from him show at once that he has not lost his old-time understanding of them. /

" 'Dixie Land,' which is really the proper name of the song, was written by Emmett in 1859, while he was a member of the celebrated 'Bryant's Minstrels,' which then held forth at No. 472 Broadway, in New York City. His engagement with them was to the effect that he should hold himself in readiness to compose for them a new 'walk-around' whenever called upon to do so, and to sing the same at the close of their performance. The

circumstances attending the composition of 'Dixie'
are interesting: One Saturday night after a performance Mr. Emmett left the hall and was proceeding homeward when he was overtaken by Jerry
Bryant and asked to make a 'hooray' and bring it
to the rehearsal Monday morning. Mr. Emmett
replied that it was a short time in which to make a
good one, but that he would do his best to please
Mr. Bryant. He composed the 'walk-around' next
day, Sunday, and took it to the rehearsal Monday
morning, music and words complete. The tune
and words of 'Dixie' as now sung are Mr. Emmett's
exactly as he then wrote them. At times different
aspirants for its authorship have been cut short in
their attempts to lay claim to it by the timely inter-
ference of friends of the composer."

The following is the full text of the original
son, as written by Mr. Emmett:

I wish I was in de land ob cotton, old times dar are not
    forgotten;
    Look away, look away, look away, Dixie land!
In Dixie land whar I was born in, early on one frosty
    mornin',
    Look away, look away, look away, Dixie land!

CHORUS.

Den I wish I was in Dixie, hooray! hooray!
In Dixie land I'll took my stand, to lib and die in Dixie.
Away, away, away down south in Dixie!
Away, away, away down south in Dixie!

Ole missus marry "Will-de-weaber"; Willum was a gay
    deceaber;
Look away, look away, look away, Dixie land!
But when he put his arm around her, he smiled as fierce as
    a forty-pounder;
Look away, look away, look away, Dixie land!

His face was sharp as a butcher's cleaber, but dat did not
    seem to greab her;
Look away, look away, look away, Dixie land!
Ole missus acted de foolish part, and died for a man dat
    broke her heart;
Look away, look away, look away, Dixie land!

Now here's health to de next ole missus, an' all de gals dat
    want to kiss us;
Look away, look away, look away, Dixie land!
But if you want to drive 'way sorrow, come an' hear dis
    song to-morrow;
Look away, look away, look away, Dixie land!

Dar's buckwheat cakes an' Injin batter, makes you fat or a
    little fatter;
Look away, look away, look away, Dixie land!
Den hoe it down an' scratch your grabble, to Dixie's land
    I'm bound to trabble;
Look away, look away, look away, Dixie land!

"Mr. Emmett has had numerous applications from many eminent people all over the country for the original copy as a curiosity, one of them coming from Mrs. General Sherman.

"From the time it was first sung at Bryant's hall in New York, it became a favorite all over the United States, as fast as minstrel troupes could bring it before the people. It is interesting to know how 'Dixie' became the Southern war song. A spectacular performance was being given in New Orleans late in the fall of 1860. Each part had been filled; all that was lacking was a national march and song for the grand chorus, a part the leader had omitted till the very last moment. A great many marches and songs were tried, but none could be decided upon. 'Dixie' was suggested and tried, and all were so enthusiastic over it that it was at once adopted and given in the performance. Immediately it was taken up by the populace, and sung in the streets, in homes and concert halls daily. It was taken to the battlefields and there established as the Southern Confederate war song. When asked what suggested the words and tune of 'Dixie,' Mr. Emmett said that when the cold wintry days of the North set in all minstrels had a great desire to go to 'Dixie's land' to escape the hardships and cold. On a cold day a common saying was, as Mr. Emmett expresses it, 'O! I wish I was in Dixie's land,' and with this as a key he concluded with the words as given above. The tune of 'Dixie' was composed in much the same way; one bar of music set the key for the immortal 'Dixie.' "

The pathetic part of Mr. Emmett's life is thus told by Mr. Bok:

"Emmett, as I have said at the beginning of this article, is now nearly eighty years old, but he is a 'young old man,' whose alertness of mind impresses one as that of a younger man. Unfortunately for him, his lot in life is not a pleasant one. Unable to work, he derives a very rude subsistence. He is practically forsaken, as well as poor. Few of the outside world know that he is alive; only the neighbors know that he is the man who, through one of his songs, moved millions of hearts and helped to fight and win many battles. He is a prophet in his own country. But this is all. Thousands who know the words of his famous song, know not the name of its composer. To all intents and purposes, he is forgotten. And, what is sadder still, he carries the hard burdens of poverty. Practically, his only present return for his song is the knowledge of the service it rendered in troublous times. Yet, it seems to me, that this man ought not to be entirely overlooked by the nation which he served so well."

It was not long after the New Orleans incident that the tune of "Dixie" became widespread in its popularity, and other words were written to fit the measure. As early as May 30th, 1861, Albert Pike, then of Arkansas, (born in Boston in 1809,) published in The Natchez Courier a song which

was frequently used in the Confederate army, and
is, perhaps, the most meritorious of all the words
set to that stirring tune:

> Southrons, hear your country call you!
> Up, lest worse than death befall you!
> To arms! To arms! To arms, in Dixie!
> Lo! all the beacon fires are lighted—
> Let all hearts be now united!
> To arms! To arms! To arms, in Dixie!
>   Advance the flag of Dixie!
>   Hurrah! Hurrah!
> For Dixie's land we take our stand,
> And live or die for Dixie!
>   To arms! To arms!
> And conquer peace for Dixie!
>   To arms! To arms!
> And conquer peace for Dixie!
>
> Hear the Northern thunders mutter!
> Northern flags in South winds flutter!
>   To arms!
> Send them back your fierce defiance!
> Stamp upon the accursed alliance!
>   To arms!
>   Advance the flag of Dixie!
>
> Fear no danger! Shun no labor!
> Lift up rifle, pike, and sabre!
>   To arms!
> Shoulder pressing close to shoulder,
> Let the odds make each heart bolder!
>   To arms!
>   Advance the flag of Dixie!
>
> How the South's great heart rejoices,
> At your cannons' ringing voices!
>   To arms!

For faith betrayed, and pledges broken,
Wrongs inflicted, insults spoken,
        To arms!
    Advance the flag of Dixie!

Strong as lions, swift as eagles,
Back to their kennels hunt these beagles!
        To arms!
Cut the unequal bonds asunder!
Let them hence each other plunder!
        To arms!
    Advance the flag of Dixie!

Swear upon your country's altar
Never to submit or falter!
        To arms!
Till the spoilers are defeated,
Till the Lord's work is completed.
        To arms!
    Advance the flag of Dixie!

Halt not till our Federation
Secures from earth's powers its station!
        To arms!
Then at peace, and crowned with glory,
Hear your children tell the story!
        To arms!
    Advance the flag of Dixie!

If the loved ones weep in sadness,
Victory soon will bring them gladness.
        To arms!
Exultant pride soon vanish sorrow;
Smiles chase tears away to-morrow.
        To arms!
    Advance the flag of Dixie!

General Pike was an able lawyer, a poet of excellent repute, a philologist of no mean ability,

and at one time was the highest Masonic dignitary
in the United States. He was a veteran of the
Mexican war, and became a brigadier general in
the war between the states. A few years after the
surrender he removed to Washington, where he
engaged in the profession of law; but retired in
1880, and devoted himself to literature. He published many volumes, including his poems, law re-
ports, "Masonic Statutes and Regulations," and
"Morals and Dogma of Free Masonry;" and at his
death in Washington, on the 1st of April, 1891,
he left eighteen volumes of manuscript without a
single blemish or erasure.

Another song set to the tune of "Dixie," and
which became very popular in the South, appeared
anonymously in The Charleston Mercury almost
simultaneously with General Pike's poem. It was
called "The Star of the West," and ran as follows:

I wish I was in de land o' cotton,
Old times dar ain't not forgotten—
    Look away, look away, lads in gray!
In Dixie land whar I was born in,
Early on one frosty mornin'—
    Look away, look away, lads in gray!
    (Chorus—Den I wish I was in Dixie.)

In Dixie land dat frosty mornin',
Jis 'bout de time de day was dawnin'—
    Look away, look away, lads in gray!

De signal fire from de East bin roarin',
Rouse up, Dixie, no more snorin'—
    Look away, look away, lads in gray!

Dat rocket high a-blazing in de sky,
'Tis de sign dat de snobbies am comin' up nigh—
    Look away, look away, lads in gray!
Dey bin braggin' long, if we dare to shoot a shot,
Dey comin' up strong and dey'll send us all to pot.
    Fire away, fire away, lads in gray!

Fanny J. Crosby, the blind hymnist, whose
gospel songs are popular in all English-speaking
countries, wrote words to the music of "Dixie,"
which began:

"Oh! ye patriots to the battle,
    Hear Fort Moultrie's cannon rattle;
Then away, then away, then away to the fight!"

It is a very good song, but never was adopted by
the Union army, and was seldom used in the homes
of the people in the North.

So far as I can learn, Mr. Emmett never
clearly interpreted the name which is inseparably
connected with his famous song. What did he
mean by the word "Dixie" as applied to the South?
Newspapers have attempted to supply the informa-
tion, but there is a wide disagreement among them.
One writer in The Chicago Times-Herald—M. L.
Rayne—says:/ "Dixie did not originate in the
South, as is popularly believed, but was in use in
Northern circuses that had traveled in the South

and enjoyed Southern warmth and hospitality.
When the cold winds of the Northern states blew
through the circus tents the boys would shiver and
say; 'I wish I was in Dixie,' Dixie being the dimin-
utive for Dixon—south of Mason and Dixon's
line." The readers will probably remember that
Mason and Dixon's line was established by two
Englishmen—Charles Mason and Jeremiah Dixon
—in 1763-67. They were commissioned by the
British government to survey the boundary line
between Maryland and Pennsylvania, which was
made to extend westward from the Delaware river
245 miles. The line drawn by these two astron-
omers and surveyors became known as "Mason and
Dixon's line," and was made famous in the history
of the United States as the dividing line between
the free and the slave states. Whether Mr.
Emmett used this word "Dixie" in that sense can
be only conjectured.

An article in The New York Musical Age says
that Dixie was a Long Island farmer, and at his
farm, runaway negroes always found shelter and
kind treatment. Many times before the war a
wife would escape to this blissful place; then, in
the mysterous way known only to negroes, the
whisper would run from mouth to mouth that she
was in "Dixie land," and you can imagine what the

song was to that husband as he toiled in the lazy
sunshine waiting for a chance to join her.

The Century Cyclopedia of Names states that
"Dixie land" is said to have been originally a
negro name for New York or Manhattan Island,
and later applied to the South. The phrase
originated in New York very early in the century,
and when it developed into a song, or rather into
many songs, the refrain usually contained the word
"Dixie," or "Dixie Land." It is claimed, also,
that the name first came into use when Texas was
admitted into the Union in 1845, and that the
Negroes sang of it as "Dixie."

In Bryant's "Songs from Dixie's Land" is a
note to the effect that in the popular mythology of
New York City, Dixie was the negro's paradise on
earth in times when slavery and the slave trade
were flourishing in that quarter. Dixie owned a
tract of land on Manhattan Island, and also a large
number of slaves; and the slaves increasing faster
than the land, an emigration ensued such as has
taken place in Virginia and other states. Naturally, the Negroes who left it for distant parts
looked to it as a place of unalloyed happiness, and
it was the "old Virginny" of the Negroes of that
day. Hence "Dixie" became synonymous with an
ideal locality combining ineffable happiness and

every imaginable requisite of earthly beatitude.

The music of "Dixie" is so pleasing to the people that it has become almost a universal tune without words. As a piece of national music it holds a place close to "Yankee Doodle." It may be hardly more than a jig, as the Confederate officer called it, but there is in it that indefinable quality that made it alluring from the commencement of its career. And in the war with Spain, in far off Manila, in the battles around Santiago, in the camps in Porto Rico, in marches by land, in travels by sea, the soldiers were cheered by the strains of "Dixie." Its beginning was in the minstrel show, it was dedicated as a battle song in the great uprising of the South, and in its last estate it has a place among the enduring music of the Union.

James R. Randall.

XIX.

Maryland, My Maryland.

JAMES RUSSELL LOWELL pronounced "Maryland, My Maryland," the finest poem (not a song) which the civil war produced. Some may regard this as too high praise, but the fact remains that it is one of the most refined and artistic poetical productions of the war between the states, and has given lasting fame to its author— James Ryder Randall.

Some one has said that every song has what may be called a personal history, or if the expression is preferable, a secret history. Therefore, when a poet has written a war lyric which has literary finish, and qualities that make it live, no matter on what side were his sympathies in that memorable contest which displayed the supreme valor of the American soldier, the readers of the

story of those strange times, and the lovers of good
literature, have a fervent wish to know something
of the heart experience that inspired it.

Mr. Randall was born in Baltimore on the first
day of 1839. A part of his college education was
received at Georgetown, District of Columbia. A
year or two before the war broke out he went to
New Orleans and became a contributor to The
Daily Delta. He afterwards accepted the position
of professor of English literature in a small college
at Pointe Coupée, in Louisiana, about one hundred
miles above New Orleans. He was at the college
in April, 1861, when he read in The Delta that the
Sixth Massachusetts infantry had been attacked
while marching through the streets of Baltimore on
their way to the South. I will now let Mr.
Randall tell the interesting personal history of his
song as communicated to Mr. Brander Matthews,
for The Century Magazine :

"This account excited me greatly ; I had long
been absent from my native city, and the startling
event there inflamed my mind. That night I
could not sleep, for my nerves were all unstrung,
and I could not dismiss what I had read in the
paper from my mind. About midnight I rose, lit
a candle, and went to my desk. Some powerful
spirit appeared to possess me, and almost involun-

tarily I proceeded to write the song of 'My Maryland.' I remember that the idea appeared first to take shape as music in the brain—some wild air that I cannot now recall. The whole poem was dashed off rapidly when once begun. It was not composed in cold blood, but under what may be called a conflagration of the senses, if not an inspiration of the intellect. I was stirred to a desire for some way of linking my name with that of my native state, if not 'with my Lord's language.' But I never expected to do this with one single, supreme effort, and no one was more surprised than I was at the widespread and instantaneous popularity of the lyric I had been so strangely stimulated to write. The next morning the poem was read to the college boys, and at their suggestion it was sent to The Delta, in which it was first printed, and from which it was copied into nearly every Southern journal. I did not concern myself much about it; but very soon, from all parts of the country, there was borne to me, in my remote place of residence, evidence that I made a great hit, and that, whatever might be the fate of the Confederacy, the song would survive it."

The following is the poem in full:

The despot's heel is on thy shore,
    Maryland!
His touch is at thy temple door,
    Maryland!
Avenge the patriotic gore
That flecked the streets of Baltimore,
And be the battle queen of yore,
    Maryland, my Maryland!

Hark to thy wandering son's appeal,
    Maryland!
My mother state! To thee I kneel,
    Maryland!
For life and death, for woe and weal,
Thy peerless chivalry reveal,
And gird thy beauteous limbs with steel,
    Maryland, my Maryland!

Thou wilt not cower in the dust,
    Maryland!
Thy beaming sword shall never rust,
    Maryland!
Remember Carroll's sacred trust,
Remember Howard's warlike thrust,
And all thy slumberers with the just,
    Maryland, my Maryland!

Come, for thy shield is bright and strong,
    Maryland!
Come, for thy dalliance does thee wrong,
    Maryland!
Come to thine own heroic throng
That stalks with liberty along,
And give a new key to thy song,
    Maryland, my Maryland!

I see the blush upon thy cheek,
    Maryland!
But thou wast ever bravely meek,
    Maryland!

But, lo, there surges forth a shriek!
From hill to hill, from creek to creek,
Potomac calls to Chesapeake,
    Maryland, my Maryland!
Thou wilt not yield the Vandal toll,
    Maryland!
Thou wilt not crook to his control,
    Maryland!
Better the fire upon thee roll,
Better the blade, the shot, the bowl,
Than crucifixion of the soul,
    Maryland, my Maryland!
I hear the distant thunder hum,
    Maryland!
The old line's bugle, fife and drum,
    Maryland!
She is not dead nor deaf nor dumb—
Huzza, she spurns the Northern scum!
She breathes, she burns! She'll come, she'll come!
    Maryland, my Maryland!

When a great lyric has been born in such a time
as that described by Mr. Randall, there always
comes a desire to voice it in song. "Music is the
universal language of the soul." It was in the
following June that a glee club held a meeting at
the Baltimore home of Miss Hetty Cary, who
afterwards became the wife of Professor H.
Newell Martin, the distinguished biologist and
author at Johns Hopkins University. Miss
Cary's home was the gathering place of many
Baltimore sympathizers with the cause of the
South, and it was for the purpose of considering

the ways and means of assisting the Confederacy
that the club held the meeting which became so
memorable in its results. Miss Cary had read
"Maryland, My Maryland," in the papers, and
when her sister, Miss Jenny, who had charge of the
program, searched hopelessly for something to sing
which would encourage and fire the Southern
heart, Miss Hetty began to recite the poem in a
tone earnest and eloquent, when her sister
exclaimed, "Lauriger Horatius," and in a few
moments the burning words had found their mate
and that night, "Maryland, My Maryland"—to
use an expression of Alexander H. Stephens, the
Confederate vice-president—became "the Marseillaise of the Confederacy." "Lauriger Horatius" is said to be a German composition, and for
some time had been popular as a college tune.

A story is related that shortly after the words
of the song were inherently wedded to the music
at the home of the Cary's, in Baltimore, a remarkable scene occurred at Manassas, the famous battle-
field of Bull Run. While visiting friends in the
army the two sisters were serenaded by the now
celebrated Washington artillery of New Orleans.
When the band ceased playing, one of the officers
exclaimed, "Let's hear a woman's voice." Miss
Jenny Cary, standing in the front door, sang,

"My Maryland." The refrain was speedly taken
up by hundreds of Southern soldiers, and from
that moment the verses grew into a power. It was
the birth of the song in the army.

Touching the Southern heart to fervent
enthusiasm, "Maryland, My Maryland," was to
the South what "John Brown's Body" was to the
North. The popularity of each was instantaneous
and intense. No song of the South so shared the
glory of "Dixie" as did "Maryland, My Maryland." Guards who patrolled the city of Baltimore, during the war, have said that in many a
home, supposed to be neutral, at midnight and with
suppressed zeal, they heard the ruffled music of the
song.

Colonel Randall, by which title he is now
known among the Southern people, lives at
Augusta, Ga. Recently he visited Savannah, and
was serenaded by the First Maryland regiment
band, and I cannot close the story of "Maryland,
My Maryland," more appropriately than by quot-
ing from The Savannah Press, of the 9th of
January, 1899, a portion of a personal tribute to
him :

"He is a poet who has no living equal on this
side of the Atlantic, and his 'Maryland, My Maryland' stands out as the most beautiful war lyric of

modern times.   If it had been written in a
Northern state, during that stirring period,
Colonel Randall would have been idolized like
Whittier and Lowell.   It is impossible to read it
even now in the cool aftermath of the civil war
without feeling the fine frenzy which stimulated
poets and people at that time.   James R. Randall
is a man of lovable character and of loyal traits.
Maryland should make him a 'patron saint.'   No
one ever thinks of the state without recalling the
poem, and Baltimore lost her brightest genius when
she allowed Randall to wander into Georgia.   If
Edgar Poe had not already won the primacy for
Maryland in poesy and letters, James R. Randall
would have secured it for that state; for Randall
has immortalized the name of Maryland.   The
poem was written in Louisiana and published in
The New Orleans Delta, and Randall awoke one
morning to find himself famous.   The stirring German tune, 'Tannenbaum,' was chosen as the fitting
accompaniment of 'Maryland.'   It was after the
battle of Manassas that some Maryland ladies
visited the headquarters of General Beauregard,
and sang 'Maryland, My Maryland.'   The soldiers
caught up the refrain and the whole camp rang
with the soulful melody.   From that time 'Maryland' became a national war song in the South."

XX.

The Bonnie Blue Flag.

DURING the exciting days of the civil war when songs played an important part in quickening the steps of the army and stimulating courage, the "Bonnie Blue Flag" was very useful in the South, but today it is hardly more than a remembrance of those troublous times. James R. Randall's native modesty led him to say in a letter to Mr. Brander Matthews, quoted in The Century Magazine, that "Dixie" and the "Bonnie Blue Flag" were the two most popular songs of the Confederacy. The latter did have a large "run" during the heat of the conflict, but when the war ended and the cause of the South was lost, there was nothing either in the words or music of the song to make it a worthy memento of the fated struggle through which the Southern people had patiently and intrepidly passed.

The melody of the "Bonnie Blue Flag" is of Irish origin, and is said to have been composed, or rather adapted, by Henry McCarthy. One authority says he was a Scotch actor, while another writes of him as an Irish comedian. There is no doubt that the air is purely Irish as it is very evident that it was taken from the "Irish Jaunting Car." There is also a conflict of statement as to the time the song was first sung. The weight of authority, however, renders it reasonably safe to say that it was first given to the public at the Variety theater in New Orleans, during the latter part of 1861. The "Bonnie Blue Flag" became very popular throughout the South, and in New Orleans it was sung so frequently and with such perplexing enthusiasm by the Southern sympathizers, that when General Butler had possession of the city in 1862, he issued an order which imposed a fine of twenty-five dollars upon every man or woman who should be heard singing or playing it. In addition to this penalty, all the copies of the song that could be found were destroyed, and publishers were prohibited from printing it in any form. That the readers may understand the bright spirit and swinging movement of the song, I give it in full:

We are a band of brothers and native to the soil,
Fighting for our liberty with treasure, blood and toil,
And when our rights were threatened the cry rose near and
    far—
Hurrah for the Bonnie Blue Flag that bears a Single Star.

CHORUS.

Hurrah, hurrah, for Southern rights hurrah!
Hurrah for the Bonnie Blue Flag that bears a Single Star.

First, gallant South Carolina nobly made the stand;
Then came Alabama, who took her by the hand;
Next, quickly Mississippi, Georgia and Florida,
All rais'd on high the Bonnie Blue Flag that bears a Single
    Star.

Ye men of valor, gather round the Banner of the Right,
Texas and fair Louisiana, join us in the fight;
Davis, our loved president, and Stephens, statesman rare,
Now rally round the Bonnie Blue Flag that bears a Single
    Star.

And here's to brave Virginia! the Old Dominion State
With the young Confederacy at length has linked her fate;
Impell'd by her example, now other states prepare
To hoist on high the Bonnie Blue Flag that bears a Single
    Star.

Then cheer, boys, raise the joyous shout,
For Arkansas and North Carolina now have both gone out;
And let another rousing cheer for Tennessee be given,
The Single Star of the Bonnie Blue Flag has grown to be
    Eleven.

Then here's to our Confederacy, strong we are and brave,
Like patriots of old, we'll fight our heritage to save;
And rather than submit to shame, to die we would prefer,
So cheer for the Bonnie Blue Flag that bears a Single Star.

The general opinion is that Mr. McCarthy wrote the words, but one author gives the authorship to Mrs. Annie Chambers-Ketchum, who was one of the most popular poets in the South at the breaking out of the war. She was born in Kentucky in 1824. Her husband, who was an officer in the Confederate army, was severely wounded at the battle of Shiloh, in April, 1862, and died from the effects thereof the following year. She wrote many poems which were published in the book form, and is also the author of several works on teaching, and has made many translations from the Latin, German and French. Mrs. Ketchum, who is now living in New York City, does not claim the authorship of the song which has been ascribed to her.

A prominent Southern writer, himself a poet of high order, writes me under the date of January 31, 1899: "I cannot give you any definite statement about the words of the 'Bonnie Blue Flag.' I suppose Henry McCarthy is as much entitled to the authorship as anybody. As a bit of verse it is mere drivel and trash. I do not know of any self-respecting literary person who would father or mother it."

The government at Washington has done a praiseworthy work in procuring for the new

library of Congress, a collection of Confederate
music—that is to say, music printed in various
parts of the South during the civil war. Some of
these songs are reprints from music preceding the
war. "Her Bright Smile Haunts Me Still,"
"Good-by, Sweetheart," "Call Me Not Back From
the Echoless Shore," and many of Foster's
melodies are among the collection. There is the
famous pathetic anthem, "Lorena," which had a
large run in the Confederacy. "Maryland, My
Maryland," is in two forms—one lithographed
handwriting on flimsy paper, and the other somewhat more ambiguous, printed in Augusta and
certified to as being the "only edition that has the
author's approval."

One Confederate anthem has for a frontispiece
a cavalier holding the Southern standard,
inscribed, "God Save the South." There is a
ballad of the times called "Pray, Maiden, Pray!
Pray for the Southern Land of Streams and Sunlit
Pines;" a song of "The Southern Soldier Boy,"
to the tune of "The Boy with the Auburn Hair;"
a "Virginia Marseillaise," calling "Brothers True
to Guard on the Trenchant Brand;" a Southern
adaptation of "When This Cruel War is Over,"
and, likewise, "Who Will Care For Mother Now?"
anthems that came at the end of the war, indica-

tive of the impatience of both sides for the close of the strife. There is also a "Farewell Forever to the Star-Spangled Banner," which was to have been supplanted "by thirteen bright stars around the palmetto tree;" "The Bonnie Blue Flag" and "All Quiet Along the Potomac Tonight," attributed to Lamar Fontaine.

These are all entered for copyright in the "District Court of the Confederate States of America," and form an interesting relic of the "lost cause."

Henry Carey.

r

XXI.

Great Britain's National Anthem.

O NE of the most potent national anthems in existence is "God Save the Queen." It seems to be the product of no man and of no time. Its words are few and simple, but there is a power in them that not many national songs possess. Its greatness is measured by its influence upon forty millions of people, by the love of country it inspires, and by its universal use among the inhabitants of the United Kingdom.

As much "history" has been written of "God Save the Queen" as of "Yankee Doodle," but whether anyone has ever given the correct story of the words and music is uncertain. The essential question, "By whom were they written, and when?" has never been satisfactorily answered. It would seem to be easier to trace the sources of the Nile than to discover the true history of the

British national anthem. One account says that
the music originated with John Bull, a noted
musician, organist to James I. in 1607, and afterwards organist of the Cathedral of Antwerp, where
he died in 1628. In support of this theory it is
said that among the manuscript volumes of compositions, by Dr. Bull, was found an organ
voluntary identical in rhyme with "God Save
the King," and "bearing considerable resem-
blance to it in the form of its melody." In
an old Christmas Carol, printed at Aberdeen,
in 1682, are found phrases very much like the
present national anthem of Great Britain, and
therefore the claim is put forth that the music
has a Scottish origin. There is also a story that
the melody, and stanzas of similar construction to
"God Save the King," appeared in France, in
1686, during the reign of Louis XIV., and was
long associated with the vintages of old France.

The commonly accepted history of the words
and music is that they are the work of Henry
Carey, a poet and musician, who was born about
1685, and apparently died by his own hand in
1743. He wrote innumerable songs and witty
poems, and the production by which he is best
known is "Sally in our Alley." But imputing to
him the authorship of either the words or melody

has provoked much controversy; but nevertheless, it is asserted by some historians that it was first performed by Carey as his own composition—words and music—at a public banquet in London, in 1740, to celebrate the taking of Porto Bello, on the Northern shore of the Isthmus of Panama, by Admiral Vernon, November 20, 1739. The anthem was first published about 1742 or 1743, in the Harmonica Anglicana, and in the Gentleman's Magazine, in 1745. These are some of the points set forth in the long and tiresome discussion of the origin of the song, but no one has been able to clearly establish the authenticity of anyone of the claims.

In Moore's Cyclopedia of Music—a work edited with painstaking care—is the following brief story of the tune which has such a hold on the world:

"It has been generally believed that Henry Carey was the author, and that he employed Dr. Thornton, of Bath, and Christopher Smith, Händel's clerk, to correct the words as well as the music. This gave rise to the assertion that Händel was the composer. The words with the air appeared in the Gentleman's Magazine, in 1745, when the landing of young Stuart called forth expressions of loyalty from the adherents of the

reigning family. After Dr. Arne (composer of
the popular hymn tune 'Arlington,' and the song
'Rule Britannia') had brought it on the stage, it
soon became very popular. Since that time the
harmony of the song has been much improved, but
the rhythm is the same as originally. There is
a story that this national song was not made for
King George, but that in the older versions it ran
'God Save Great James, our King,' and that it was
originally written and set to music for the Catholic
chapel of James II., and no one durst own or sing
it after the abdication of James, fearing to incur
the penalty of treason, so that the song lay dormant
sixty years before it was revived for George II.
It is very interesting to observe how this song of
which the words have no great merit, has become
dear to the whole English nation, on account of the
associations connected with it."

William T. Stead, that great lay preacher of
political and social righteousness, and editor of
The London Review of Reviews, prints in his
valuable little book, "Hymns that have Helped,"
a story of the origin of "God Save the Queen."
This much can be said in favor of the story—it is
interesting, and may be as true to history as anything that Richard Grant White, or anyone else,
has written on the anthem that has been the hope

and despair of many writers. Mr. Stead says:
"It is one of the ironies of history that the first
trace that can be discovered of the singing of the
English national anthem, imploring Divine help
for the reigning monarchy, was an occasion when
its petitions was most conspicuously refused. In
1688, when William of Orange was busy with his
preparations in aid of the conspiracy against the
Stuart dynasty, a Latin chorus was sung in the
private chapel of James II., which appears to have
been the origin of the famous anthem. But before
the year was out, it was King James who was sent
packing, and William of Orange reigned in his
stead. Then, as if to keep up the irony, the song
disappeared altogether until the Pretender in
1745 attempted, by the aid of his faithful Scots, to
regain the crown his ancestors lost. Then the
self-same musical prayer, first used, unavailing, on
behalf of James II., was revived in order to serve
as the Battle Hymn of the usurper who sat upon
his throne. Twelve days after the proclamation of
the Pretender in September, 1745, at Edinburgh,
'God Save the King' was sung with tremendous
enthusiasm at Drury Lane, and from that hour to
this it has held the first place among the national
anthems of the world."

There is a wonderful attractiveness in the

simple melody to which "God Save the Queen" is sung. Beethoven introduced it in his "Battle Symphony," and Weber has used it in three or four of his compositions. It is a tune striking enough to become international. It is popular in France and Prussia, and Denmark and Sweden have set it to national songs. It was also the state melody of Russia for many years until the Czar Nicholas, not being pleased with an imported air, concluded that his people should sing a national hymn from Russian heart and brain, and in 1833 Lwoff composed the tune of "God Preserve the Czar," which, wedded to new words, is the best of all the peculiar national anthems of that country. The melody of "God Save the Queen," by an accident more than otherwise, became indissolubly linked to "My Country, 'tis of Thee."

The following is the form in which England's national anthem has been sung since the beginning of Victoria's reign:

> God save our gracious Queen!
> Long live our noble Queen!
>   God save the Queen!
> Send her victorious,
> Happy and glorious,
> Long to reign over us,
>   God save the Queen!

O Lord, our God, arise.
Scatter her enemies,
    And make them fall!
Confound their politics,
Frustrate their knavish tricks,
On her our hopes we fix,
    O, save us all!

Thy choicest gifts in store
On her be pleased to pour,
    Long may she reign!
May she defend our laws,
And ever give us cause,
To sing with heart and voice,
    God save the Queen!

The song has found its way into some hymnals in England, and possibly would have had a universal welcome in British hymn books had it not been for the fourth and fifth lines in the second stanza, which are not only rough and queer, but intrinsically ridiculous. Many have wondered why some first-class hymn-mender has not taken the matter in hand and made a stanza equally as fine and singable as the first and the last. But no one has been inclined to disturb the sentiment of a national anthem which has been such a power for one hundred and fifty years. Mr. Stead says that no part of this battle hymn of the British monarchy is more genuine and hearty than the stanza which offends many pious critics on account of the fidelity with which it reproduces the spirit of the imprecatory Psalms of David.

The universality of the anthem is a prominent feature of its history. When the Columbian Exposition was being held in Chicago, in 1893, a number of representatives thereto, made up of twenty-seven diverse nationalities, and speaking, when at home, fifteen different languages, passed over the Canadian frontier at Gretna, in Manitoba, on August 29th, "for the purpose of heartily cheering Queen Victoria, and singing 'God Save the Queen.'" There is no other national hymn in the world that could have been sung so effectively under similar circumstances.

Only a few years ago The Youth's Companion gave an account of a dinner given a Harvard team by an English team in England; and the Harvards were requested beforehand to sing "The Star Spangled Banner," and their English hosts were to respond with "God Save the Queen." But no Harvard man, and none of their friends, knew "The Star Spangled Banner." But when the English team sang the song of which every Englishman is proud, its sentiment was as heartfelt as the volume of sound was majestic.

Better than anything I can say as to the spirit and purpose of "God Save the Queen," are a few words from Mr. Stead: "The singing of the national anthem, and the way it was sung in January, 1896, when England, left in 'splendid' but dangerous 'isolation,' was preparing for war against envious rivals in Europe and America, did more than anything else to impress the foreign observer with the intensity and depth of the national emotion. It was magnificent, almost awful, to hear the swelling notes as they rose from great congregations. For more than a hundred years, whenever the English people have been really stirred by imminence of national danger, or by exultation over national triumphs, the most satisfying expression for their inmost aspirations has been found in the simple but vigorous verse. This is the war song of the modern Englishman. For him it has superseded all others, ancient or modern. 'Rule Britannia' is not to be compared with it for universality of use, or for satisfying completeness of verse and music.

"Whenever any number of Englishmen find themselves fronting death, or whenever they have experienced any great deliverance, whenever they thrill with exultant pride, or nerve themselves to offer an unyielding front to adverse fate, they have used 'God Save the Queen,' or King, as it has been, and will be again, as the natural national musical

vehicle for expressing what would otherwise find
no utterance. It is the melody that is always
heard when our island story touches sublime
heights or sounds the profoundest depths. It is
one of the living links which bind into one the past,
the present, and future of the English race."

Rouget de Lisle.

XXII.

The Marseillaise.

FRANCE has produced some of the most entrancing patriotic hymns the world has ever heard. These lyrics have gone to the hearts of the people and have seemed to speak to millions as to one man. The French are a singing nation, and they sing as they fight, and we are told that "to the sound of songs monarchy fell to pieces in France at the close of the eighteenth century."

"Carillon National" was a song revolutionary in its spirit, and was the favorite air of Queen Marie Antoinette. But she lived "to hear it sung as a cry of rage and hatred against herself; it pursued her to the cell, and startled her on her way to trial; and the beautiful, but ill-fated and misguided queen, heard its harsh strains coming from the vast multitude in inexpressible insolence as she

lay her head under the guillotine." The supreme
tragedy of the French Revolution was inaugurated
with a song from the opera of "Richard Cœur de
Lion"—Richard the Lion-Hearted—the words
being applied to the despot, Louis XVI., and the
scenes which followed are among the bloodiest in
all modern history.

Claude Joseph Rouget de Lisle was born at
Lons-le-Saulnier, France, in 1760. He became a
captain of engineers, and was stationed at Strasburg in 1792. War had been declared against the
Austrians, and the fate of France seemed to
tremble as if in a balance. The mayor of Strasburg became acquainted with De Lisle, and on the
24th of April, 1792, he invited the young engineer
to dine with him, and knowing that he had a turn
for music and poetry, asked him to write a martial
song to be sung on the departure of six hundred
volunteers who had been called to join the army
of the Rhine, and which would also rouse a higher
spirit of patriotism among the people of the city,
that Strasburg might be the better able to resist
an attack by the Austrians. Excited by the dinner
and complimented by the invitation, De Lisle, who
was intensely fiery and emotional, produced, before daylight the following morning, what Ulbach
calls "the eternal poem of the great apogee of the

Revolution." There was an unconscious conjunc-
tion of the hour and the men, and in an outburst
of patriotic frenzy the immortal national song of
France was born:

> Ye sons of freemen, awake to glory,
>   Hark, hark what myriads bid you rise,
> Your children, wives, and grandsires hoary,
>   Behold their tears and hear their cries!
> Shall hateful tyrants, mischief breeding,
>   With hireling hosts, a ruffian band,
> Affright and desolate the land,
>   While peace and liberty lie bleeding?
>   To arms! To arms, ye brave!
>   Th' avenging sword unsheath!
>   March on, march on, all hearts resolved
>   On liberty or death.
>
> Now, now the dangerous storm is scowling
>   Which treacherous kings, confederate, raise;
> The dogs of war, let loose, are howling,
>   And, lo! our fields and cities blaze.
> And shall we basely view the ruin,
>   While lawless force, with guilty stride,
> Spreads desolation far and wide,
>   With crimes and blood his hands embruing?
>
> With luxury and pride surrounded,
>   The vile, insatiate despots dare,
> Their thirst of power and gold unbounded,
>   To mete and vend the light and air;
> Like beasts of burden would they load us,
>   Like gods would bid their slaves adore;
> But man is man, and who is more?
>   Then, shall they longer lash and goad us?

O Liberty! can man resign thee!
  Once having felt thy gen'rous flame?
Can dungeon, bolts, and bars confine thee,
  Or whips thy noble spirit tame?
Too long the world has wept, bewailing
  That falsehood's dagger tyrants wield;
But freedom is our sword and shield,
  And all their arts are unavailing.

When it was sung in the public square the next
day it excited so much enthusiasm that nine hundred, instead of six hundred, volunteers joined the
army for the Rhine. The song of the "Marseillaise" was startling. "It was the fire-water of the
French Revolution," and evoked fierce passions
and terrible deeds. The inflaming accents of the
song drove men to crimes more desperate than we
can comprehend to-day. In "The Story of a Musical Life," Dr. George F. Root says that when he
was in Paris, on the Fourth of July, 1851, he and
five other Americans thought they would celebrate
the day. They had a big dinner, and speeches, and
songs. They sang "The Star Spangled Banner,"
and "America;" and finally they agreed to compliment the French, and Dr. Root began the "Marseillaise," "Ye sons of freedom, wake to glory;"
but he had not gone far, when the lady of the house
rushed into the room, frantic in speech and wild
in demonstration, commanding them to stop the

"Marseillaise," for a crowd was collecting, and her house would be in ruins. And, sure enough, the song had been heard upon the street, and a vast throng was preparing to charge upon the rooms from which had come the blood-stirring words and tune. An old soldier, who served under the First Napoleon, boarding at the same place, went down to the street and explained the good intentions of the innocent Americans, and after much persuasion the crowd dispersed. The "Marseillaise" had been interdicted for many years by the French government because of fear respecting its effect upon the passions of that inflammable people.

In 1830, Heinrich Heine, the most prominent figure in German literature since Goethe and Schiller, wrote of the "Marseillaise:" "What a song! It thrills me with fiery delight, it kindles within me the glowing star of enthusiasm and the swift rocket of desire. Swelling, burning torrents of song rush from the heights of freedom in streams as bold as those with which the Ganges leap from the heights of the Himalaya! I can write no more, this song intoxicates my brain; louder and nearer advances the powerful chorus:

'To arms! To arms, ye brave!'"

Rouget de Lisle named the song "The War

Song of the Army of the Rhine." But in a few
months it found its way to Marseilles, and to other
cities in France, and was extensively used by enthusiastic revolutionists. On the 30th of July,
1792, it was first sung in Paris by a horde of
ruffians from Marseilles—"five hundred strong,
the vilest and most brutal of the floating popula-
tion of a Mediterranean sea-port town, who were
summoned to Paris for the purpose of exciting and
assisting at the atrocities of 1792." The Parisians
called it "the song of the Marseilles," and as such
it became the official hymn of the republicans of
France.

The extraordinary character of the air has
given it a more eventful career than any other song
that ever was born of a call to battle. It has been
"the signal of destruction, the warning note of
revolution." When the song was only seven
months old—November, 1792—the republicans of
France, under Dumouriez, fought the Austrians
at Jemappes, in Belgium. At the most perilous
hour in that great battle, Dumouriez, finding that
his right wing was almost without officers, and
giving way before the fire of the Austrian infantry, put himself at the head of his army, and began
to sing the "Marseillaise" hymn. The soldiers
joined in the song, their courage was redoubled,

they charged the enemy, and the victory placed
Belgium in the power of France.

"During the Crimean war before Sebastopol,
a body of French troops were detached to storm
the Malakoff. The line was formed and at the
signal they moved to the charge. The Russians
met them and hurled them back. Again they re-
formed and rushed with impetuous daring upon
the foe, and again were repulsed. Seven times
they advanced, and seven times the thinned and
enfeebled ranks were driven before the Russians.
They rallied the eighth time and called for the
'Marseillaise.' But the soldiers refused to move
until the music sounded. The inspiring strains
rose over the frightful carnage of the bloody field ;
the men shouted for the onset, and madly rushed
through blazing showers of shot and shell. Whole
ranks were mowed down ; their places were filled
from the rear, and louder than the storm of battle,
above the wild outcry, 'March on ! March on !'
rang the triumphant and immortal song of France.
The men leaped the trenches, and inspirited by the
song which dispelled all fear, and inspired the
climax of courage, they plunged into the furnace
of fire and death, drove the Cossocks from their
guns, and the Malakoff was won."

When Rouget de Lisle wrote the "Marseillaise," he little thought to what base use it would be put, or what would be his own fate. He was as loyal as any man in France, but being suspected of being disloyal, he was imprisoned during the Reign of Terror in Paris, and heard his song above the roar of battle in the storming of the Tuileries on the 10th of August, 1792; but when Robespierre fell, De Lisle was released. He would have gone to the guillotine with the "Marseillaise" ringing in his ears, had not a happy circumstance set him free before his fatal turn came. Soon after Rouget de Lisle was proscribed as a Royalist, he fled from France and took refuge in the Alps. And Richard Grant White says "the echoes of the chord that he so unwittingly had struck, pursued him even to the mountain tops of Switzerland." "What," he said to a peasant guide, "is this the song I hear—

'Ye sons of France, awake to glory?'"

And it was upon the wilds of the mountains, whither he had been driven by a frenzy which he had innocently incited, that he first learned that his "War Song of the Rhine" had become the song of the Marseilles.

Rouget de Lisle was wounded, with many other Royalists, at Quiberon, in France, in 1795, and after quitting the army he was reduced to sordid poverty for many years; and it was not until 1830, six years before his death, that Louis Philippe granted him a pension.

XXIII.

Battle Hymns of Germany.

A VAST array of illustrations of battle songs in history is found in Germany. In the story of war lyrics of that country we meet with "flashing, sword-cut songs and fierce epics which read like the rush of a torrent of blood amid the groans of the dying, formulating battle hymns no less dominant than they were among the Norsemen who lived to sing and sang to die." From the fifteenth century to the present day, the songs of Germany have risen with almost every generation in fresh swarms. If we take a retrospect of German life, we will find the people of that country, most prone, perhaps of all modern races, to outbursts of feeling in song. A Spaniard or a Frenchman sings as if he could not help it; a German sings as though he would not help it if he could. This accounts for the earnest spirit

Max Schneckenburger.

of so many of their songs of the Reformation, and the cultured and well-balanced form or even their rudest soldier songs. The consequence has been that the German-folk, not being ashamed of poetic expressions of their feelings, have done all honor to their poets, and have sung their war songs enthusiastically and in triumphant tones. The agonies of Germany in the Thirty Years' war and other conflicts, produced up to the end of the seventeenth century 32,700 patriotic and Christian songs. Such an unburdening of the emotions of the heart and of the conflict of the soul in song can scarcely find a parallel in the history of any other race of people.

Germany has produced some war ballads which roused the masses to the highest pitch of excitement. In the uprising of the German nation in 1813, Theodor Körner, born in 1791, encouraged his comrades in the army by writing fiery, patriotic songs. He was an enthusiastic patriot, and the night before the battle near Rosenburg, which was fought on the 26th of August, 1813, and in which he was killed, he wrote his famous "Sword Song," which for some time was regarded as the "Marseillaise" of the German people.

One of Germany's most powerful battle songs came from the heart of Ernst Moritz Arndt, who

was born in 1769, and died in 1860. The year
1813 is memorable in the history of Germany's
struggle for liberty. The country had been involved in the war by Napoleon, and when his Russian campaign had resulted disastrously, the remnant of his once great army, famished and frozen,
"wandered like ghosts across the snowfields of Germany looking for shelter."

During those trying times, faithful preachers
of the gospel of political liberty traveled over Germany, gave the people patriotic songs to sing, en-
couraging them to trust in God, and to have con-
fidence in a free and united Germany.

When Napoleon had fled from Russia, making
his way to Paris, two men could be seen in a sleigh
hurrying toward the Russian frontier with a message of hope to patriotic Germans in the field.
They were Baron Stein, the noted constitutional
authority, and the poet Arndt, whose songs became
as powerful as the sword. It was during this winter's ride that Stein, after having been long
absorbed in thought, exclaimed: "The Prussian
congress must be convened; the volunteers must
be called out—Austria, Saxony, Westphalia, Bavaria, Wurtemberg, Tryol—and so the rest of Germany must follow in the wake."

Arndt, also, was equal to the occasion, and

shouted in response: "Das Ganze Deutschland soll es sein—My country must be all Germany. You have the constitution, but I have the song of German liberty." And that enthusiasm gave birth to the magnificent song which did so much to inspire the army with courage and to win the battle that made Germany free and united. "What is the German Fatherland?" is the leading line in each stanza. "Is it Prussia, is it Saxony, is it Bavaria!" and so on, to which each stanza answers "No, no, no." Poultney Bigelow, in Harper's Magazine, says that "Arndt, following the logic of Stein, on that frosty sleigh ride amid the wreck of Napoleonic armies, ends his song with the immortal words—'Das Ganze Deutschland soll es sein—My country must be all Germany.'" The power of that song in the mighty struggle of Germany for liberty in 1813, can never be fully measured.

Another of Arndt's great war songs was "What is the German Fatherland?" It was a product of the time when Thiers began to stir up France to war with Germany. It was powerful enough to muster the German people as one man. It was a cry of defense and vengeance that probably has never been equalled. The song remains to this day one of the great national songs of Germany, and whether "trolled out by a booted and spurred trooper, or by a company of rollicking sailors, it is always an incentive to action, and sometimes to deeds of heroism."

These rousing times in Germany gave birth to a "Rhine Song," written by Nicolaus Becker. In the sense of being a well-constructed lyric, it was not as great as others which preceded it, but happily and rhythmically, it expressed the fixed determination of the German heart to hold the Rhine against the power of France, and its effect was something marvelous. It is claimed that it was set to music by seventy different composers.

The chief patriotic song of Germany is "Watch on the Rhine," but the national hymn which "thrills the whole German empire is "Heil Dir im Siegerkranz"—"Hail to Thee in the Conqueror's Wreath." It was written in 1790 as a song for the birthday of Christian VII. of Denmark, by Heinrich Harries. When it passed into Berlin in 1793, it was recast into its present form by Balthasar Gerhard Schumacher, and sung to the tune to which we sing "My Country, 'tis of Thee," and from which it has never been separated. This national hymn has such a strong hold on German affection that the centenary of its publication was celebrated with demonstration and enthusiasm throughout the Empire in December, 1893.

It would seem that Germany, in her struggle with France, had little need of more patriotic songs. She had already a dozen living, moving, exciting battle hymns. But every new phase of every conflict which fired the German heart produced a new song. It was in 1840 that Max Schneckenburger, then twenty-one years old, wrote his potent and wonderful "Watch on the Rhine." He was not a poet, but a hustling, every-day business man; but from his soul, as from a flint, leaped the spark which made Germany one flame of patriotism. When he saw the left bank of the Rhine threatened by France, his heart was more than ever warmed with a love of home and country, and in a moment of great emotion he sang, as one translation gives it:

> "The Rhine is safe while German hands,
> Can draw and wield the battle-brands,
> While strength to point a gun remains,
> Or life-blood runs in German veins."

There are many English translations of the "Watch on the Rhine," but the one which has been most highly commended is found in Warner's Library of the World's Best Literature, and is as follows:

A voice resounds like thunder peal,
'Mid dashing wave and clang of steel;
"The Rhine, the Rhine, the German Rhine!
Who guards to-day my stream divine?"

CHORUS.

Dear Fatherland! no danger thine,
Dear Fatherland! no danger thine;
Firm stand thy sons to watch, to watch the Rhine,
Firm stand thy sons to watch, to watch the Rhine.

They stand a hundred thousand strong,
Quick to avenge their country's wrong;
With filial love their bosoms swell;
They'll guard the sacred landmark well.

While flows one drop of German blood,
Or sword remains to guard thy flood,
While rifle rests in patriot's hand,
No foe shall tread thy sacred strand!

Our oath resounds, the river flows,
In golden light our banner glows,
Our hearts will guard thy stream divine,
The Rhine, the Rhine, the German Rhine!

The power of this song was so great that it was
afterwards seized by four eminent composers—F.
Mendel of Berne, in 1840; Leopold Schroter of
Warlitz, in 1852; F. W. Sering of Strasburg, in
1852; and last, and greatest of all, Carl Wilhelm of
Schmalkalden.   The words of "Watch on the
Rhine" were first sung to Wilhelm's melody on
the 11th of June, 1854.   Schneckenburger died in
1849, long before his song became famous, as it

did not attain widespread popularity until the breaking out of the Franco-Prussian war. It then became the song of the mightiest army of modern Europe, and, in fact, the pean of all Germany; and nothing could resist the song of the Rhine in the defense of that country against the attacks of France.

Emperor William, recognizing the influence of the melody of "Watch on the Rhine" on the German army, gave Wilhelm a pension of $750 a year, and when he died, two years later, his native city erected a handsome monument to his memory.

It has been said that every important turn in the fortunes of war in Germany—"the repulse of Wallenstein from Stralsund, the frightful devastation of Magdeburg, the battle of Lützen, the death of Gustavus Adolphus—each memorable action, whether advance or retreat, has been recorded in song." But it was not until the beginning of the present century, when the great struggle began for the union of all that was "home-born and Teutonic," that Germany's battle songs became "truly splendid." It was indeed in the lyrics of Körner, Arndt, Becker and Schneckenburger that German patriotism reached its culmination. These were true poets of the soul, and, to borrow a sentence from Amelia E. Barr, "their products

have become part and parcel of that rich inherit-
ance of song that so nobly interprets the intense
love of freedom and unaffected simplicity of the
German character."

General Index.

www.ingramcontent.com/pod-product-compliance
Lightning Source LLC
Chambersburg PA
CBHW020339030726
47496CB00007B/1944